A Kaleidoscope
of Identities

A Kaleidoscope of Identities

Reflexivity, Routine, and the Fluidity of Sex, Gender, and Sexuality

James W. Messerschmidt and Tristan Bridges

ROWMAN & LITTLEFIELD
Lanham • Boulder • New York • London

Published by Rowman & Littlefield
An imprint of The Rowman & Littlefield Publishing Group, Inc.
4501 Forbes Boulevard, Suite 200, Lanham, Maryland 20706
www.rowman.com

86-90 Paul Street, London EC2A 4NE

British Library Cataloguing in Publication Information Available

Library of Congress Cataloging-in-Publication Data

Names: Messerschmidt, James W., author. | Bridges, Tristan, author.
Title: A kaleidoscope of identities: reflexivity, routine, and the fluidity of sex, gender,
    and sexuality / James W. Messerschmidt and Tristan Bridges.
Description: Lanham: Rowman & Littlefield, [2022] | Includes bibliographical
    references.
Summary: "This book proffers a new conceptual framework of sex, gender, and sexual
    identity, presenting data that documents these identities as typical and extensive rather
    than exceptional. A Kaleidoscope of Identities reveals the more elusive elements
    of sex, gender, and sexual life which are often difficult to capture in quantifiable
    variables"—Provided by publisher.
Identifiers: LCCN 2022012003 (print) | LCCN 2022012004 (ebook) | ISBN
    9781538167861 (cloth) | ISBN 9781538167878 (paperback) |
    ISBN 9781538167885 (ebook)
Subjects: LCSH: Gender identity. | Sex role. | Sex. | Identity (Psychology)
Classification: LCC HQ18.55 .M47 2022 (print) | LCC HQ18.55 (ebook) | DDC
    305.3—dc23/eng/20220311
LC record available at https://lccn.loc.gov/2022012003
LC ebook record available at https://lccn.loc.gov/2022012004

Contents

Preface

In her article "'Said and Done' versus 'Saying and Doing': Gendering Practices, Practicing Gender at Work," Martin (2003) argues that practicing gender is an active phenomenon, accomplished quickly, directionally, in interaction with others, and routinely with liminal awareness. For example, she reports on an interaction between Tom and Betsy, both vice presidents in a Fortune 100 company, who stood

> talking in a hallway after a meeting. Along the hallway were offices but none was theirs. A phone started to ring in one office and after three or so rings, Tom said to Betsy, "Why don't you get that?" Betsy was surprised by Tom's request but answered the phone anyway and Tom returned to his office. (Martin 2003, 346)

Afterward, Betsy confronted Tom by stating: "I'm a vice-president too, Tom, and you treated me like a secretary. What were you thinking?" Tom responded, "I did not even think about it" (2003, 346). Martin analyzes how the shape of the unequal encounter was hidden from both participants in the interaction. Although Betsy eventually recognized the inequality, her participation initially remained invisible to her, and Tom did not recognize at all what he did prior to being confronted. Both Betsy and Tom were participating *routinely*, yet *unreflexively*, in an instance of a localized, dominating form of ephemeral hegemonic masculinity (Messerschmidt 2018a).

Tom clearly controlled the situation by directing Betsy to answer the phone, and initially, Betsy complied—with neither, at the outset, recognizing the interaction as gendered. In this instance, the social construction of culturally supported dominating "masculine" qualities (commanding and controlling) in unequal relation to culturally supported subordinate "feminine" qualities (obedience and submission) *routinely* transpires, producing hegemonic masculinity, emphasized femininity, and unequal gender relations. Although Tom and Betsy unintentionally and spontaneously contributed to the construction of gender hegemony (Messerschmidt 2018a), Martin points out that neither engaged reflexively:

They did not analyze the situation; they were "practiced" in gender; they practiced gender. The gender institution holds women accountable to pleasing men; it tells men/boys they have a (gender) right to be assisted by women/girls; Tom and Betsy knew this. Tom's request and Betsy's behavior are thus unsurprising. Without stopping to reflect, Tom practiced a kind of masculinity that the gender institution makes available to him, which is to request practical help from women; Betsy responded in kind by complying with his request. (2003, 346)

Tom's and Betsy's interaction did not require reflexivity because, as Martin argues, "Tom's request made perfect sense to both" (2003, 347). Tom and Betsy engaged in routine gendered social interaction and identity work that did not necessitate deliberate forethought or a reflexive strategy.

Martin argues that routine accomplishments of gender embodied by both Betsy and Tom (the "said and done") provided a framework for them to miss this moment in the social construction of unequal relations between them (the "saying and doing"). For Martin, this example represents gender practice as more routine than reflexive. Yet, she also reports another situation wherein Tom engaged in gender *reflexivity*. Tom had developed a personal policy that he reflexively followed for thirty years of never having dinner with a woman with whom he works:

Many years ago, . . . when I first started working, uh, I made a rule to myself that I would never have dinner with a woman alone, just the two of us. And, to be quite honest, I said I never want to be in a position where either I would be tempted, or anyone could come in and see [us] and develop a wrong impression. So, I have breakfast with them [women], and I would have lunch, but I would never have dinner alone with a woman. Just a rule. (Martin 2003, 348)

In other words, through internal deliberation, Tom *reflexively* developed a gendered "rule" of refusing to have dinner alone with a woman with whom he is working. The rule demonstrates reflexivity about gender identity and inequality. Yet, Tom assumes his rule "protects" women (and his own reputation) when in fact it also works to structurally offer women fewer opportunities to network and to build the kinds of professionally close relationships with superiors and possible mentors that could lead to valuable opportunities (e.g., Valerio and Sawyer 2016).

Martin's (2003) article is both useful and unusual in defining and differentiating *routine* and *reflexive* gender practices. Martin's (2003, 2006) work was pioneering in our conception of gender practice, concentrating on what she labeled "gender practices" and "practicing gender." The former refers to embodied practices "available" in specific social settings for individuals "to enact in an encounter or situation in accord with (or in violation of) the gender institution" (2003, 354). The latter entails gendered social action often accomplished quickly, directionally (in time), unreflexively, routinely, informed by liminal awareness, and through interaction with others. Although Martin conceptualized practicing gender as more routine than reflexive, she notes that a thorough understanding of gender practice requires attention to agency, intentionality, awareness, and the role of reflexivity in its daily constitution. This book responds to that call by theorizing not simply reflexivity but the symbiotic relationship between reflexivity and routine in the construction of sex, gender, and sexual identities.

Despite this, the dichotomy of gender practice illustrated by Tom—one routine and one reflexive—is the convention when both are discussed by sociologists in their research and theorizing. Sociologists tend to study social practice as exclusively or primarily accomplished *either* routinely *or* reflexively, although (as discussed in "The Past") theorizing gender has been less susceptible to that criticism than have other subfields. Yet, the dynamic relationship between routine and reflexivity is undertheorized. Sociologists often miss the *coexistence* of reflexivity and routine in sex, gender, and sexual practice and identity formations.

Rather than interrogating gender practice as *either* routine *or* reflexive, in "Identity Reminiscences" we present data from life-history interviews with two individuals, Jessie and Morgan (both pseudonyms), that document routine and reflexive sex, gender, and sexual identities as typical and extensive rather than exceptional. Throughout their life courses, Jessie and Morgan— who both eventually identified as genderqueer—constructed kaleidoscopic sex, gender, and sexual identities through a symbiotic nexus between routine and reflexive practices (conditioned by context) that provide useful illustrations of the new conceptual framework outlined in "Theory and Method" (for further information on "genderqueer" as an identity, see Nestle, Howell, and Wilchins 2020; Richards, Bouman, and Barker 2017; Worthen 2020).

Contemporary theoretical tools in sociology hinder an understanding of the dynamic interplay between reflexivity and routine in the formation of sex, gender, and sexual identities. To remedy this, we follow the lead of feminist sociologists in examining the relationship among situational interaction, accountability, and relational and discursive social structures to address sex, gender, and sexual practice as *both* reflexive and routine. This perspective and the data presented demonstrate reflexivity and routine in a more symbiotic relationship than has been acknowledged in the past. Without privileging either, we explore this relationship by examining the ways reflexivity and routine collaboratively shape sex, gender, and sexual identities over the course of Jessie's and Morgan's lives.

In this book, then, we apply a new conceptual framework of sex, gender, and sexual identity formation to the life histories of Jessie and Morgan. These two cases were part of a small set of fourteen interviews completed by the lead author in 2010 and 2011 with white, working- and middle-class genderqueer young adults, all of whom were assigned female at birth, and who now associate with sex, gender, and sexual expansive communities and identities. Although not a representative sample, the two case studies reveal the more elusive elements of sex, gender, and sexual life that are often difficult to capture in quantifiable variables. Both of these life stories deepen and augment our understanding of how eventual sex, gender, and sexual identities are related to reflexive and routine practices and, thus, personal life history.

Importantly, we do not represent Jessie's and Morgan's life stories as exemplars of becoming genderqueer—such identities are wide ranging and involve numerous ways of embracing this identity. Instead, we present their life histories as nuanced case studies that demonstrate our conceptualization of the symbiotic relationship between reflexivity and routine in the formulation of mutually—yet variably—constituted sex, gender, and sexual identities. We use the term "becoming" in a different way, as the process of formulating a new identity. Identities are continually in the midst of becoming; they undergo a gradual course of transformation into a new identity, in particular, as social context changes. And the identified kaleidoscopic identities of Jessie and Morgan were embedded in their reflexive and routine practices as well as the changing social contexts in which they participated, leading eventually to the construction of differing forms of a genderqueer identity.

A Kaleidoscope of Identities: Reflexivity, Routine, and the Fluidity of Sex, Gender, and Sexuality opens with "The Past" which summarizes and examines some of the most influential feminist theories and research formulated since the 1970s and 1980s. The discussion concentrates on sociological feminist theories that ignore reflexivity and/or routine practices, as well as theories and research that include a conceptualization of either reflexivity or routine, and feminist sociological scholarship that recognizes both reflexive and routine practices. None of these feminist perspectives, however, examines the interconnections between reflexive and routine sex, gender, and sexual identities. "The Past" concludes by arguing that our new conceptual framework builds on these perspectives by analytically conceptualizing the symbiotic relationship between reflexivity and routine practices and how such practices are particularly associated with the variable mutual constitution of sex, gender, and sexual identities.

"Theory and Method" presents a novel theoretical framework—what we label "structured action theory"—for conceptualizing sex, gender, and sexual practices and identities. To understand the social construction of sex, gender, and sexuality, we must first grasp what has been understood as the "doing" and "determining" of sex, gender, and sexuality. Following this, "Theory and Method" discusses how the theory conceptualizes the "doing/determining" of sex, gender, and sexual identities in relation to each of the following:

the symbiotic link between reflexivity and routine; reflexive and routine embodiment; structured action; sex, gender, and sexual hegemony; and non-hegemonic sexes, genders, and sexualities. "Theory and Method" closes with a brief discussion of the methodology of the study from which the two life stories of Jessie and Morgan are drawn.

"Identity Reminiscences" applies the conceptual framework of sex, gender, and sexual identities outlined in "Theory and Method" to the life histories of Jessie and Morgan. Both Jessie and Morgan, at the time of the interviews, self-identified as genderqueer, which they conceptualized as meaning either that they consider themselves to be *both* masculine and feminine (Jessie) or *neither* masculine nor feminine (Morgan). Although genderqueer people express their sex, gender, and sexual identities in a variety of ways, they are similar in the sense that such identities are transgressive, thereby challenging the hegemonic binary constructions of sex (male/female), gender (masculine/feminine), and sexuality (heterosexuality/homosexuality), and thus represent one example of the new nonhegemonic sexes, genders, and sexualities identified in "Theory and Method." "Identity Reminiscences" summarizes Jessie's and Morgan's life stories from their earliest memories during childhood family dynamics to their attendance at university.

Finally, "The Future" discusses the data presented in "Identity Reminiscences" in the context of the theoretical framework proposed and, in the process, suggests future research directions for sex, gender, and sexuality scholars. We conclude the book with a summary and analysis of the key findings and correspondingly provide suggestions for prospective and subsequent scholarship.

ACKNOWLEDGMENTS

Heartfelt thanks to Pat Martin. From the beginning of this project, Pat was an enthusiastic and important participant who provided immense help in analyzing one of the life histories presented here (Jessie). Unfortunately, for personal reasons Pat was unable to continue working on this venture and thus had to drop out. As discussed earlier, Pat's classic article published in 2003 was the inspiration for this undertaking, and we thank her for the significant insight she has contributed to this book.

James extends significant thanks to Tristan, whom he met at a conference where they discussed Tristan's important work on the sociology of masculinities, and they became fast intellectual friends. James and Tristan have worked together on several projects in the past, and like these other projects, working on this book as coauthors has been a wonderfully respectful, supportive, and collaboratively intellectual relationship throughout. James also expresses considerable appreciation to the entire staff at Rowman & Littlefield—his favorite publisher!—but especially to Jon Sisk (one of the top acquisitions editors in the business!), Sarah Sichina (assistant editor), Anna Keyser (production editor), and Nancy Syrett (copyeditor). Most of all, James thanks Ulla, Erik, and Jan for everything they have done to support him—they are the most important people in his life!

Tristan gratefully acknowledges James for inviting him to work together on this project. After meeting initially at a summer conference of the American Sociological Association just after Tristan received his PhD, James has been an incredibly compassionate and enduring source of inspiration, support, mentorship, and friendship. Tristan also thanks Jon Sisk and the staff and production team at Rowman & Littlefield, particularly for tolerating Tristan wanting to spend more time with the manuscript. Tristan also thanks Verta Taylor, France Winddance Twine, Beth Schneider, and Geoff Raymond for discussions of this project and for their support. He thanks Amy and Mike for their friendship and support throughout the pandemic, along with Reagan and Sidney. And finally, Tristan thanks his family, Tara, Ciaran, and Desmond, whom he loves above all else.

Although we present a new and fresh analysis in this book, some of the material included herein has appeared elsewhere in different forms, growing out of earlier publications. The book includes a revision of certain parts of chapter 1 and a complete revision of chapter 5 from James W. Messerschmidt's *Hegemonic Masculinity: Formulation, Reformulation, and Amplification* (Lanham, MD: Rowman & Littlefield, 2018). The two life stories were previously published in James W. Messerschmidt's *Masculinities in the Making: From the Local to the Global* (Lanham, MD: Rowman & Littlefield, 2016) but are republished here with a completely novel commentary and analysis.

The Past

To understand the interplay between *reflexive* and *routine* gendered practices and identities, it is helpful to first distinguish between "patriarchy" and "gender." In the 1960s, existing social theory was either sex blind or attributed "sex inequality" to the alleged "inferior nature" of women. Theorizing "patriarchy" was initially undertaken by feminist scholars in response to traditional androcentric social theory, and feminists adapted different meanings of the concept. Not long after the emergence of feminist theories of patriarchy, however, feminist scholars began to argue that the concept presented significant problems, especially regarding gender agency and practice.

In "The Past", we first summarize the two most notable feminist theories utilizing the concept of patriarchy in the 1970s: radical feminism and socialist feminism. We then summarize the critiques of "patriarchy" articulated predominantly in the late 1970s and throughout the 1980s. Among the major criticisms was the accurate position that both radical and socialist feminism were arguably deterministic in the sense that behavior was seen as simply resulting from a social system—either "patriarchy" or "patriarchal capitalism"—external to social actors themselves. In such a view, individuals display little or no agency; rather, their social practices are framed as resulting directly from the structure of patriarchy or patriarchal capitalism. Radical and socialist feminism, then, failed to account for the choices people make, for the intentions of social actors, and for how social action is a meaningful construct in itself.

What grew out of these criticisms was a major shift in theoretical focus in feminist theory—from "patriarchy" to "gender." We examine the shift in language from a focus on "patriarchy" to one centrally concerned with "gender." With that change, new conceptual frameworks emerged that highlighted *gender practice*, and thereby additionally stressed choice, intent, and routine social action during the construction of gender identities. We briefly summarize the two most influential feminist sociological theories that emerged during the late 1980s—by Raewyn Connell (1987) and Candace West and Don Zimmerman (1987)—and how both examined choice and routine as separate yet crucial to gender practice.

1

Next we summarize scholarship from a collection of feminist sociologists of gender who, in the 2000s, became interested in scrutinizing reflexive and routine gender practices. Although this work is insightful, reflexivity and routine were seen as separate, theoretically privileging gender practice as *either* more routine than reflexive *or* more reflexive than routine. Building on this work, we argue that conceptualizing reflexivity and routine as interconnected helps us appreciate, study, and understand this relationship in a new and more dynamic way. We conclude "The Past" by summarizing the work of a few feminist sociologists who have worked within Pierre Bourdieu's framework by combining reflexivity with *habitus*. Although this scholarship is an advance on work that concentrates exclusively on either reflexive or routine practices, Bourdieu's notion of *habitus* is a contested theoretical concept that we argue is less *sociologically* helpful than is sometimes assumed—mainly because of its emphasis on the unconscious—in theorizing routine gendered practice. We build on this work to fully capture the symbiotic relationship between reflexivity and routine practice.

"The Past" is essential to the discussion herein because we build on this body of theory and research to conceptualize reflexivity and routine as interconnected—and thus, not analytically or theoretically separable in ways they often are treated—by arguing that it is their coexistence and interplay that shape gender practice and identities. But first, we summarize the debate that led feminist scholars to shift from an emphasis on "patriarchy" to investing in theorizing "gender."

FROM "PATRIARCHY" TO "GENDER"

In this section, we summarize first the two most notable feminist theories utilizing the concept of "patriarchy" in the 1970s: radical feminism and socialist feminism. A simple distinction between the two theories is instructive: radical feminists turned to the concept of patriarchy to refer exclusively to power relations between men and women, while socialist feminists attempted to analyze not simply patriarchy but, rather, how patriarchy and capitalism interact to construct specific kinds of power relations between men and women. Following a summary of this body of work, we discuss the criticisms of both attempts to theorize patriarchy articulated in the late 1970s and throughout the 1980s. Such critiques included the fact that both theories were structurally deterministic and thus had not conceptualized reflexivity and/or routine practices as shaping gender relations and inequality. What grew out of these criticisms was a major shift in theoretical focus in feminist theory—from "patriarchy" to "gender." Indeed, this shift is perhaps less appreciated than it ought to be as it was a dominant conversation among feminist theorists around the world. We conclude by outlining this change. The shift from patriarchy to gender as the primary theoretical object in feminist theory led to an articulation of agency in different ways and, eventually, an awareness of and focus on the relationship between reflexivity and routine in gender practices.

Prior to the emergence of the concept of *gender*, feminist theories of the 1970s illuminated the patterns of power between men and women that social theory to that point had all but ignored.[1] In particular, it was "radical feminism" and "socialist feminism" that actually put second-wave feminism on the academic map. These theories secured for sexual politics a permanent role in popular culture and the academy and moved analysis of power between men and women to the forefront of feminist thought and analysis.

Radical Feminism

The goal of radical feminism was to understand the power of men in society and to develop appropriate strategies for its elimination. Radical feminism viewed the power and privilege of men—what came to be known as *patriarchy*—as the root cause of all forms of social inequality. Patriarchy, within this perspective, was seen as primary, meaning that all other social relations (such as class, race, age, and sexuality) derive from relations and inequality between women and men. For radical feminists, women were, historically, the *first* oppressed group and thus patriarchy—alleged by radical feminists to exist in every known society—is the most widespread and deepest form and structure of oppression. According to radical feminism, history is an ever-changing struggle of men for power and domination over women, this being the "dialectic of sex" (Firestone 1970). Radical feminism made distinctive and original contributions to feminist theory but also—as we discuss in more detail—became entangled with biological arguments regarding the foundation of patriarchy. In what follows, we briefly summarize the development of radical feminism because this hitherto history is significant for understanding the eventual formulation of theories concentrating on gender.

Second-wave feminism was stimulated by Simone de Beauvoir's well-known argument in *The Second Sex*: "One is not born but rather becomes a woman." As de Beauvoir points out: "biological fate" does not "determine the figure that the human being presents to society; it is civilization as a whole that produces this creature indeterminate between male and eunuch which is described as feminine" ([1949] 1972, 295). De Beauvoir argues that the social—not the biological—determines women's situation; that is, women are embedded socially in unequal patriarchal relations where they are compelled "to assume the status of Other" (29). "Women," according to de Beauvoir, are quite literally constructed as a social class under patriarchy. It is not biology that determines women's destiny, "but the manner in which her body and her relation to the world are modified through the action of others than herself" (734).

Among the early academic feminists to take de Beauvoir's work seriously was Kate Millett (1970) in her book *Sexual Politics*. Millett theorizes "politics" as "power-structured relationships, arrangements whereby one group of persons is controlled by another" (1970, 23) and applies this definition to make sense of unequal relations between women and men. Millett explicitly theorizes power relations between women and men as "patriarchy," which she maintains did not dissolve with the emergence of a market economy. According to Millet, power relations between men and women are "sturdier than any form of segregation, and more rigorous than class stratification, more uniform, certainly more enduring," situating patriarchy as "the most pervasive ideology of our culture and provid[ing] its most fundamental concept of power" (25). She continues: "Our society, like all other historical civilizations, is a patriarchy," a form of societal organization whereby "that half of the populace which is female is controlled by that half which is male" (25). In *Sexual Politics*, patriarchy is presented as a universal phenomenon, and every avenue of power within contemporary society—the military, the economy, the educational system, the state, and so on—is seen as entirely under the control of men. In short, the power of men permeates the entire society, and patriarchy is the social structural base of all power relations—racial, sexual, political, and economic.

Millett further argues that though patriarchy manifests itself throughout society, the family is its chief institution. Through sex role socialization, the family operates to encourage members to adjust and conform to patriarchal ideologies and practices. Human personality is formed along lines of "masculine" and "feminine," lines that entail an elaborate, dichotomous, and oppressive code of conduct through which men are viewed as possessing superiority and, accordingly, are allocated public and private power. As Millett (1970, 26) further argues, the creation of such "sex roles" constructs a binary involving aggression, intelligence, force, and efficacy among men; passivity, ignorance, docility, virtue, and ineffectuality among women. And with regard to specific practices, such sex roles "assign domestic service and attendance upon infants to the female, the rest of human achievement, interest, and ambition to the male" (26). Millett rejects biological reductionism, arguing that men and women are trained to accept a social system divided into "male" and "female" spheres, encompassing unequal power relations.[2]

Millett emphasizes power in the *private* realm because, for her, the foundation of patriarchy is the private and interpersonal power by which men dominate women. For Millett, this private realm was best articulated by examining heterosexual couples and family life. Whereas all previous social analyses had concentrated on the *public* nature of power in terms of class, caste, and status, Millett argues that personal relations between men and women were soundly political, similar to domination and subordination in politics generally. This domination by men is not only enforced by naked violence, Millett argues, but occurs through sex role socialization and the personal nature of power in the home. Indeed, the most durable forms of inequality have been shown to be those we are socialized to understand as legitimate; for Millett, the family helped articulate the legitimacy of patriarchy as a social structure. It was radical feminists who popularized the slogan that "the personal is political," the idea that there exists a political dimension to personal life. Insofar as inequality is institutionalized throughout society, sex role socialization occurs in all walks of life.

Classic radical feminist works, such as Millett's, did not afford agency a central place in their theories of patriarchy. As such, radical feminist work is also subject to similar criticisms lodged against an inability of sex role theory to acknowledge and thus explain agency (e.g., Stacey and Thorne 1985; Connell 1985a, 1987). Early radical feminists argued that the normal functioning of institutions dominated by men sufficed to maintain the social control of women and to reproduce patriarchy. Nevertheless, Millett did point out that control in patriarchal society would be imperfect and even inoperable without the rule of force. In patriarchal society, then, men were perceived by Millett as being equipped psychologically and physically to perpetuate interpersonal violence against women, if necessary, to maintain power, authority, and control.

By the mid-1970s, however, the radical feminist emphasis on the social nature of patriarchy and the learning of gender was considered an unsatisfactory idealist explanation of men's dominance, and radical feminists began to search for root causes of patriarchy (Jaggar 1983). Millett's concentration on men's social power quickly became the biological essentialism of subsequent feminist scholars. In particular, radical feminists assigned strictly dichotomous and intrinsic natures to men and women as the "root cause" of patriarchy. In the mid-1970s, the materialist alternative of biological reductionism became fashionable in much radical feminist thought (Eisenstein 1983).

Susan Brownmiller (1975) was in the forefront of adding this new twist to radical feminist theory. In *Against Our Will: Men, Women and Rape*, Brownmiller (1975) advances the idea that rape is the actual foundation of patriarchy and, therefore, propagates inequality by viciously subordinating women to men and limiting, indeed policing, women's social behavior. For Brownmiller, rape is not a *sociological* question but a *biological* one. Because humans enjoy a unique form of sexuality not based entirely on reproduction, the sexual urge can occur virtually at any time, and not simply in response to a reproductive cycle. And despite the emphasis on the "sexual urge," there was no conception of reflexivity in Brownmiller's perspective.

In addition to the unique nature of human sexuality, the body also plays a critical and determinant role in rape. Brownmiller (1975, 14) argues that had it not been for an accident of biology, "an accommodation requiring the locking together of two separate parts, penis into vagina, there would be neither copulation nor rape as we know it." Finally, Brownmiller argues that because men possess raw physical strength in relation to women, they make use of this physical ability to overcome their biological sexual urge. It is the combination of this biological and physical capacity to rape that leads men to construct an "ideology of rape." In short, "when men discovered that they could rape, they proceeded to do it" (14). But we never learn what the process actually involves by men in constructing an ideology of rape and how specifically men decide to take up that ideology.

This ability and resulting ideology to rape became simultaneously the mechanism of controlling women and a weapon of force against them. From prehistoric times to the present, according to Brownmiller (1975, 15), rape has played a crucial role in reproducing patriarchy: a "process of intimidation by which *all men* keep *all women* in a state of fear." The fear created by sexual violence has, according to Brownmiller, acted historically and cross-culturally as a means of social control. For Brownmiller, although all men are potential rapists, not all men need to engage in rape for patriarchy to be sustained. The men who do rape provide the necessary means for maintaining patriarchy. Brownmiller concludes that on the shoulders of rapists "there rests an age-old burden that amounts to an historic mission: the perpetuation of male domination over women by force" (209). Brownmiller sees rapists as the "front-line shock troops . . . in the longest sustained battle the world has ever known" (209). This sexual violence is, for Brownmiller, the personal political weapon sustaining patriarchy and the subordination of women. In fact, it was Brownmiller who initially popularized the idea that "rape is violence, not sex," subsequently adopted by other feminists.

Brownmiller's perspective differs from Millett's and other early 1970s radical feminists in the sense that patriarchy is not a sociological phenomenon but, rather, is founded in biological differences between men's and women's bodies. Brownmiller argues that because rape and women's subordination seemed to exist in every known society, patriarchy is a universal system that stems from biological causes and, thus, "men" and "women" are no longer social categories constructed through socialization.[3]

Brownmiller differs from early radical feminists in another important way: in her work, sexual violence against women was seen, for the first time, as central to radical feminist theorizing. It was now clearly asserted by radical feminists that violence against women is the foundation of patriarchy, and therefore, sexual danger replaced sexual pleasure as a central component of radical feminist thought. Despite such differences, Millett and Brownmiller did show a similar perspective in the sense that men and women are depicted as distinctly different categories from each other.

In traditional social thought, women were the Other, the different, inferior, and deviant category. For many radical feminists of the mid- to late 1970s (and throughout the 1980s), "femaleness" was increasingly theorized as normative, and "maleness," the Other. Rather than viewing women's difference from men as a source of their subordination, radical feminists began considering these differences as a source of pride and reason for confidence. Eventually, this position led to a celebration of an alleged essential "femaleness" and a denunciation of an avowed essential "maleness." Radical feminist theorists like Mary Daly, Robin Morgan, Adrienne Rich, Andrea Dworkin, and Catharine MacKinnon represented everything—from the workplace to the bedroom—that is "female" as good and everything "male" as bad (Echols 1989; Eisenstein 1983). For example, Rich (1976, 39, 72) argues that there are superior powers inherent in women that do not exist in men, and consequently, these powers bond women with the "natural order"; women's special powers associate her "more deeply than man with natural cycles and processes." Similarly, Hester Eisenstein (1983, 112) writes that, for these radical feminists, "women embody the force of light and men the force of darkness."

By the mid-1970s and into the 1980s, the issue of violence against women moved to center stage for radical feminism. This focus on "male" violence merged with a denunciation of "maleness" as the "force of darkness" and a new criticism of heterosexuality as a social institution, creating a condemnation of what became known as "male sexuality." In other words, heterosexuality was now explicitly theorized as the underpinning essence of patriarchy and linked with violence against women. For example, Robin Morgan (1978, 165) claimed as early as 1978 that "rape exists any time sexual intercourse occurs when it has not been initiated by the woman, out of her own genuine affection and desire." Andrea Dworkin (1980, 288) connects "male sexuality" with murder by arguing that "sex and murder are fused in the male consciousness, so that one without the other is unthinkable and impossible" and that "the annihilation of women is the source of meaning and identity for men."

This fusion of violence and heterosexuality as the mainstays of patriarchy was most theoretically developed in the work of Catharine MacKinnon. MacKinnon (1989) argues that sexuality is a natural attribute and the primary sphere of men's power, encompassing the expropriation of women's sexuality by men. It is the exploitative nature of heterosexuality that structures men and women as social beings in society. MacKinnon further claims that the universal system of patriarchy is maintained through heterosexuality and sexual violence. For MacKinnon, sexuality is crucial to women's subordination, and she theorizes it as a dynamic of inequality. The formula reads as follows: "sexuality equals heterosexuality equals the sexuality of (male) dominance and (female) submission" (MacKinnon 1989, 137). MacKinnon adds that "sexuality is the dynamic of control by which male dominance—in forms that range from intimate to institutional, from a look to rape—erotizes and thus defines man and woman, gender identity and sexual pleasure," and "maintains and defines male supremacy as a political system" (137). MacKinnon argues that intercourse is not that different from rape: "it is difficult to distinguish the two under conditions of male dominance" (174)—as heterosexuality is simply coercive and violent sex. MacKinnon concludes that if "sexuality is central to women's definition and forced sex is central to sexuality, rape is indigenous, not exceptional, to women's social condition" (172). Following the logic of MacKinnon's argument, *all* heterosexual women are victims, and *all* heterosexual men are rapists.

A significant change in radical feminist thought then emerged in the 1970s and 1980s: the emphasis shifted from the social nature of patriarchy through sex role socialization to biological essentialism as the base of patriarchy. This necessitated a return not only to assigning strictly dichotomous and intrinsic natures to men and women—and thus to no conception of agency and thereby reflexivity and routine practices—but also to a celebration of "femaleness" as the ultimate virtue and a condemnation of "maleness" and heterosexuality. These radical feminists upheld binary understandings of gender in biological reductionist ways, even as they attempted to reverse the moral valence associated with the social and cultural categories of "women" and "men." And it is this essential categorical difference that leads to patriarchy, which seeks to "subjugate and colonize" the "relative and powerful essence" of femaleness (Budgeon 2015, 247).

Socialist Feminism

During the early stages of second-wave feminism, other feminists working within the Marxist tradition did not follow the essentialist path and developed an alternative feminist perspective. In the mid-1960s, Juliet Mitchell (1966, 13) focused on "asking feminist questions but trying to come up with some Marxist answers." Marxist feminists—as they would become known—subsequently attempted to explain women's oppression through the use of Marxist categories, and this theoretical framework became the precursor to socialist feminism.

Marxism was viewed at the time as *the* social scientific explanation of subordination, yet that explanation had historically ignored women's labor. In particular, Marxism failed to acknowledge women's work in the home, much less comprehend how this acknowledgment would lead to a conflict theory of inequality between men and women as part of the very structure of capitalist societies. Marxist feminists began to theorize more seriously Frederick

Engels's ([1884] 1942, 76) claim that "the determining factor in history is, in the last resort, the production and reproduction of immediate life," involving "the production of the means of subsistence" and "the production of human beings themselves." For example, Margaret Benston (1969) sought to uncover the material conditions of "reproduction" that operate in capitalist societies in ways that effectively define the group "women." According to Benston, women's work in the home entails the production of "use values," not the production of marketable commodities. This production of use-values in the home, according to Benston (1969, 20), is the defining cornerstone of women, women's labor, and inequalities between men and women.

Benston and others (e.g., Seccombe 1973) were introducing women's reproductive labor in the home into an androcentric Marxist framework to demonstrate that domestic labor could be explicitly analyzed as productive work. Women's domestic segregation in capitalist economies could actually be explained, they argued, through Marxist theory. The implication was that Marxism provided the conceptual tools for establishing not only that women's work in the home is a form of *labor* but also that this type of labor is central in the explanation of the unique forms of subordination from which women suffer within capitalist societies more generally. According to these feminist theorists, then, the oppressor was theorized as the system (capitalism) that exploits and benefits from women's labor.

Marxist feminism was an important development in the evolution of socialist feminist theory. Nevertheless, in the feminist literature of the early 1970s, an explanation for men's dominance that did not focus solely on patriarchy remained undertheorized at best, and absent at worst. Criticizing Marxist theory for its inability to specifically recognize and conceptualize inequality between men and women outside of a Marxist framework, certain Marxist feminists appropriated the concept of "patriarchy" from radical feminism and attempted to use it in a nonreductionist manner to explain men's dominance and women's subordination under capitalism. For some Marxist feminists writing in the early 1970s, the term "patriarchy" seemed adequate to address the profundity and pervasiveness of men's dominance.

One of the first Marxist feminist writings to employ this concept and to juxtapose capitalism with patriarchy was Sheila Rowbotham's *Women's Consciousness, Man's World* (1973). According to Rowbotham (1973, 117), "patriarchal authority is based on male control over women's productive capacity, and over her person." Although patriarchy existed prior to capitalism, Rowbotham argues, under a capitalist mode of production, patriarchy develops a historically specific configuration. While capitalism has "whittled away" at certain aspects of men's dominance (e.g., women's labor in the market weakens the economic hold of men over women in the family), Rowbotham argues that patriarchy has still "retained the domination of men over women in society. This domination continues to pervade economic, legal, social, and sexual life" (122). In this way, Rowbotham theorizes patriarchy as transhistorical, with contemporary iterations as refracted through the economic system. Although Rowbotham theorizes patriarchy as an autonomous system of inequality, under capitalism this system becomes "an ever-present prop in time of need" (120). For Rowbotham, then, capitalism remains primary in structuring patriarchy in her theoretical explanation of men's dominance.

It was this continued concentration on the primacy of capitalism, as represented by Rowbotham's work, that eventually produced a break from Marxist feminism. Certain feminist theorists simply refused to accept the argument that relations between men and women were somehow of secondary importance to production relations. Their goal was to construct a theory that was truly socialist and truly feminist—one that undeniably required the avoidance of overstating an economic analysis at the expense of inequality between men and women.

A theoretical understanding of patriarchy provided the means to analyze relations between men and women outside Marxist categories and was a significant step toward the formulation of a more cohesive socialist feminist theory. Expanding upon Rowbotham's initial conceptualization, patriarchy eventually was theorized as a "system" with its own history and form of subordination independent of capitalism. Socialist feminists viewed contemporary Global North societies as a composite of two equally important and discrete systems—patriarchy and capitalism—neither of which was seen as more primary than the other. Socialist feminists synthesized aspects of radical feminism and Marxism into a theory that gave priority to neither capitalism (production) nor patriarchy (reproduction) but, rather, viewed them as equal, interacting and co-reproducing. Socialist feminists viewed capitalism and patriarchy as so inextricably intertwined that they were theorized as inseparable. They argued further that the social experiences of men and women are different as are their class experiences. This differing social experience shapes and limits the lives of both men and women. Zillah Eisenstein (1979) and Heidi Hartmann (1981) were notable forerunners in an attempt to connect capitalism and patriarchy, as equally interacting "dual systems," in an effort to understand men's dominance. The goal of socialist feminists was to explain theoretically the relationship between what seemed to be two relatively autonomous systems of exploitation and oppression.

Eisenstein (1979) asserts that capitalism and patriarchy have an elective affinity such that each depends on the other for survival. The two systems do not merely operate adjacent to each other but, according to Eisenstein, are in fact so intertwined as to form a mutually constituted interdependent system—"capitalist patriarchy." Eisenstein (1979, 21) argues that both capitalism and patriarchy "embody *relations of power* which define them." To understand capitalism and patriarchy in any given historical context, Eisenstein maintains that feminist theory must grasp the power relations that give them shape. Eisenstein attempts to analyze power relations in patriarchy as part of power relations in capitalism and vice versa, rather than cut off from each other, to understand the interdependence and interconnectedness of capitalist and patriarchal power relations.

Heidi Hartmann's "The Unhappy Marriage of Marxism and Feminism: Toward a More Progressive Union" (1981) likewise attempts to overcome the weaknesses of both traditional Marxism and radical feminism. Hartmann argues that throughout its history, Marxist theory had clearly remained sex blind and that radical feminism is ahistorical, insufficiently materialist, and either ignores production relations or subsumes them under patriarchal relations. Hartmann theorizes that patriarchal relations are both distinct from and independent of capitalist relations and that both capitalism and patriarchy consist of their own systems of power and hierarchy. Hartmann's theory attempts to recognize both systems without prioritizing either. Patriarchy, Hartmann argues, like capitalism, has its own material base—men's control over women's labor power—and this historically changing system of relations between women and men interacts with, but is not subsumed by, capitalist class relations. It is this interaction that leads to historically specific forms of men's dominance and women's oppression. Capitalist class relations are theorized as gender neutral, yet Hartmann argues that when they interact with patriarchal relations, the result is a particular form of men's dominance.

The Shift from "Patriarchy" to "Gender"

Despite the different usages of "patriarchy" by radical and socialist feminists, the concept provided feminists with a theoretical object for conceptualizing the dominance of men and the subordination of women (Acker 1989). By the mid-1980s, however, serious problems regarding the concept were being discussed in feminist scholarship. For example, Acker (1989, 235) specifically criticizes patriarchy "as a universal, trans-historical and trans-cultural phenomenon: women were everywhere oppressed by men in more or less the same ways," and thus radical and socialist feminism missed the historical and contemporary variations of men's dominance and women's subordination (see also Bridges and Messerschmidt 2017). For Acker, theoretical work on "patriarchy" is inadequately sociological. As she writes, "Existing theory attributed women's domination by men either to nature or social necessity rather than to social structural processes, unequal power, or exploitation" (Acker 1989, 235). This was a major shift that enabled, as Acker puts it, "questions about how gender is involved in processes and structures that previously have been conceived as having nothing to do with gender" (238).

Raewyn Connell (1985a, 264) refers to the radical and socialist feminist use of the concept of patriarchy as "categoricalism." By this she meant to convey that both radical and socialist feminist work theorized the categories of "women" and "men" "as being in no need of further examination or finer differentiation" because these theories "operate with the categories as given" and do not concern themselves "with how they come to be what they are" (264). Connell criticizes radical and socialist feminists specifically for their concentration on two uniform, opposed, and contrasting categories rather than recognizing the diversity embedded within these dualist classifications and sought to explain and understand this variety as well. A major result of the radical and socialist feminist focus on alleged differences between the categories "women" and "men" worked to direct theory away from issues that complicate and obscure differences *among* men and *among* women, such as race, age, sexuality, nationality, embodiment, and more (265).

Connell additionally argues that the concentration on patriarchy blurred the fact that men exercise unequal amounts of control over their own lives as well as the lives of women. Connell stresses that emphasizing men and women as single categories results in neglecting a great deal of the actual experiences of real men and women being subsumed under experiences said to represent the categories to which they are theorized as belonging. By focusing on the alleged differences between two categories, radical and socialist feminists failed to consider variations within; rather, the work centers on "a case pre-sumed to be normative. The results are tacitly generalized to 'women' and 'men' at large" (Connell 1985a, 265).

Regarding the radical feminist versions of patriarchy, these theorists were specifically criticized for characterizing the alleged "typical male" "as more or less unrelieved villainy and all men as agents of the patriarchy in more or less the same degree" (Carrigan, Connell, and Lee 1987, 140). Men's violence against women as a "male" instrument for purposes of maintain-ing patriarchal power was likewise criticized. Scholars argued that although radical feminists correctly claimed the effect of violence against women as a form of social and cultural *control*, it was nevertheless invalid to assume all men behave violently for the purpose of controlling women. Although some men are clearly motivated to control women through violence, not all violent men share this specific goal, and the vast majority of men are not violent against women (Beirne and Messerschmidt 2015). Radical feminism was thus denounced for simply bulldozing the complexity in which masculinity (and femininity) is situationally, and therefore differently, accomplished through-out society.

Although recognizing the gender-blind nature of Marxism, socialist feminist theory was faulted for being uncritical of the core elements of Marxist theory. The result was postulation of a capitalist system where genderless capitalists exploit genderless workers and a patriarchal system where men exploit women (Jaggar 1983). Consequently, socialist feminist theory was conceptualized as merely attempting to tack patriarchy onto an unaltered androcentric Marxist framework (Beechy 1987). In other words, socialist feminists failed to demonstrate that capitalism and patriarchy were mutually constituted "dual systems" as MacKinnon (1982, 1989) argues.

Moreover, the concept of patriarchy was criticized for restricting the theoretical exploration of historical variation in men's dominance. As discussed earlier in "The Past," Rowbotham (1981, 365) initially accepted the validity of the concept, yet later argued that the term actually obscured "the multiplicity of ways in which societies have defined gender" and implies "a structure which is fixed, rather than the kaleidoscope of forms within which women and men have encountered one another." Similarly, Brown (1988, 410) writes that "the criticism of patriarchy *per se* tends to focus upon its character as a timeless, universal tautology that always works to reduce all gender relations to an identity of male dominance that in turn cannot be explained but simply posited."

Both radical and socialist feminist theories also proceeded from an unacknowledged but race-specific and heteronormative perspective and thus tended to write out of history the existence of gender, sexual, racial, and ethnic minority groups. These theories claimed to be relevant to *all* women and men but were in fact grounded in the specific experience of white heterosexual women and men. Radical and socialist feminism constricted the possibilities of understanding how gender, class, race, sexuality, age, and nationality intersect (i.e., Dill 1988; Mohanty 1988; Spellman 1988). To be sure, feminists of color in the late 1980s and early 1990s began to articulate how gender *intersects*—not simply *interacts*—with race, class, sexuality, and nationality (e.g., Collins 1990; Crenshaw 1989; King 1988; Dill 1988; Mohanty 1988; Spellman 1988). In short, during this time period the concept of patriarchy came to be regarded as "a-historical, apolitical, homogenizing, lacking cultural specificity, too abstract, and too broad—an imprecise category not useful in understanding the gender order" (Ozyegin 2018, 235).

Finally, and most important for the intellectual concerns developed in this book, both radical and socialist feminism were arguably extrinsically deterministic in the sense that behavior was seen as simply resulting from a social system—"patriarchy" or "patriarchal capitalism"—external to the social actors themselves. In such a view, individuals display little or no agency, but rather, their social practices directly result from the structure of patriarchy or patriarchal capitalism. As such, radical and socialist feminism failed to account for the choices people reach, the intentions of actors, and how social action is a meaningful construct itself. The result was that radical and socialist feminism completely missed the significance of reflexive and routine practice in everyday life as important components structuring identity, inequality, and social interaction more broadly.

Unable to overcome the difficulties with the concept of patriarchy as utilized in both radical and socialist feminist theories, most attempts in the social sciences to more thoroughly conceptualize patriarchy came to an abrupt end in the mid- to late 1980s (Beechy 1987). Many feminists thought the concept could not be further developed in an analytically useful way and that a new approach was needed (Acker 1989). And that shift involved a change from "patriarchy" to "gender" as *the* central and primary object of feminist theory and inquiry. Oakley (1972) was one of the first feminist scholars to acknowledge the importance of "gender" by distinguishing how it is different from "sex." In her book, *Sex, Gender, and Society* (1972), Oakley defines "sex" as the biological differences between men and women (genitalia and reproductive capacities that are allegedly universal and immutable) and "gender" as the social differences associated with each sex ("masculinity" and "femininity")—differences she understood and theorized as both variable and culturally mutable. And as Budgeon (2015, 246) notes, it was culture—rather than the body—that by the mid-1980s became determining regarding the alleged differences between men and women.

This shift from "patriarchy" to "gender" involved asking new questions, such as how gender is embedded in disciplines, institutions, and people previously seen as having nothing to do with gender, such as science, the military, organizations, and men (Acker 1989). A new feminist paradigm was forming that avoided any concentration on an independent structure like patriarchy (radical feminism), and that also avoided enduring attempts (at the time) to link the "dual systems" of patriarchy and capitalism (socialist feminism). Instead, feminist scholars began to develop a framework capable of conceptualizing how social relations are *gendered*, enabling scholars to ask new questions about how "gender shapes and is implicated in all kinds of social phenomena" (Acker 1989, 77). And by concentrating on gender *practice*, agency emerged as a focus and central aspect of theoretical formulations.[4]

Raewyn Connell was one of the first feminist theorists to initiate a theory of gender rather than patriarchy. As early as 1982, Connell and colleagues produced two books that analyzed *gender relations* in families and schools (Connell et al. 1982; Kessler et al. 1982). And Connell (1985a, 266–67) began to formulate a theory with the capacity of "grasping the interweaving of personal lives and social structure" without collapsing toward the categoricalism we summarized earlier and thus biological determinism or at least some kind of biological foundationalism. She suggests that such a theory must concentrate on the constraining power of *gender relations*, "something that people fetch up against" (267). Connell suggests that the problems associated with radical feminism and socialist feminism can be solved by a theory of gender *practice*, centering on what people do in terms of practice to shape the gender relations they live, being attentive "to the structure of relations as a condition of all practice," and recognizing "the element of choice, doubt, strategy, planning, error, and transformation" (266–67). For Connell, "structure" was internally complex, yet maintained patterns of gender relations and was interwoven with social practices.

GENDER AND EMERGENT FEMINIST
SOCIOLOGICAL THEORIES

With the shift from a feminist scholarly focus on "patriarchy" to "gender" as the primary theoretical concept in feminist theory, new conceptual frameworks in sociology emerged that highlighted gender practice, and thereby provided a new framework for understanding the gendered choices people make, the intentions of actors, and their routine social action involved in the construction of gender identities—a process newly understood as one in which gendered actors were themselves active participants. In this section, we briefly summarize the two most influential sociological theories that appeared during the late 1980s—by Raewyn Connell (1987) and Candace West and Don Zimmerman (1987)—both of which examined choice and routine as separate yet crucial elements of gender practice. These two theories continue to have a major influence on social scientific research on gender, but in particular they have been crucial to securing "gender" as the major theoretical concept within feminist sociology.

Raewyn Connell

In 1987, Connell developed a fully distinct feminist sociological theory of gender. The account of gender found in her highly influential book—*Gender and Power: Society, the Person, and Sexual Politics* (1987)—was part of a wider genre of work on gender as a social structure (e.g., Agarwal 1988; Mitchell 1971; Saffioti 1978; Walby 1986). Historically, that approach to studying gender developed out of socialist feminism. And socialist feminism and the feminist structural tradition were both constructed against Marxist reductionism that situated gender as an epiphenomenon, an effect of capitalism. At odds with that, work in this tradition sought to emphasize a specific, independent dynamic of gender relations, enabling feminist scholarship to examine gender in its own right.

Within the structural feminist literature, however, there never has been a single perspective but, rather, diversity of thought on gender relations, as noted in the differing perspectives of Walby, Agarwal, Mitchell, Saffioti, and others writing in the 1970s and 1980s. Here we concentrate on Connell's theory of gender relations because her particular perspective is unique in being particularly germane to the concerns in this book. We begin with a summary of her framework in *Gender and Power.*

Connell followed the work of Mitchell (1971) and her emphasis on patriarchy as comprising multiple structures—production, reproduction, socialization, and sexuality—and initially, in *Gender and Power*, Connell concentrates on three "substructures" of gender relations: production relations (e.g., the division of labor and the distinction between unpaid and paid work), power relations (e.g., the subordination of women to men and the arrangement of masculine authority, control, and coercion), and relations of cathexis or emotional relations (e.g., emotional attachments and sexual interactions). But later in a separate text, *Gender* (first published in 2002), she expands her approach to four substructures with the addition of symbolic relations (e.g., cultural meanings and discourses).[5]

For Connell, all four substructures are logically dynamic, emphasizing a dialectical relationship between structure and practice, and highlighting the mechanisms and processes of historical continuity and change in gender relations. Connell (1987, 2014) maps gender relations society-wide through these substructures (the "gender order"[6]) as well as within specific institutions and milieus (the "gender regimes"). Connell understood the substructures comprising gender relations as fundamentally and unavoidably historical, made and remade through historical practices and processes. Indeed, analyzing the continuity or change in gender practice occurs for Connell through the dynamic relationship between the various substructures comprising gender relations and gender practices themselves. In all gender regimes, therefore, the qualities that constitute gender identities are embedded in the routine practices whereby such regimes are structured.

One example of routine practice is illustrated by the twin notions of hegemonic masculinity and emphasized femininity, which were coined and conceptualized by Connell (1987) as specific configurations of gender practice that are composed in each substructure, institution, and milieu (gender regime), and that have the effect of working to legitimate unequal gender relations between men and women, between masculinity and femininity, and among masculinities. As Connell (1987, 183) points out in *Gender and Power*: "Hegemonic masculinity is always constructed in relation to various subordinated masculinities as well as in relation to women." Both the *relational* and *legitimation* features were central to Connell's argument, involving a certain configuration of masculinity in unequal relation to emphasized femininity and nonhegemonic masculinities. Arguably, hegemonic masculinity has no meaning outside its relationship to emphasized femininity—and nonhegemonic masculinities—or those forms of femininity (not all forms of femininity) practiced in a complementary, compliant, and accommodating subordinate relationship with hegemonic masculinity. And it is the legitimation of this relationship of superordination and subordination through which the meanings of hegemonic masculinity and emphasized femininity are revealed. The emphasis on hegemony in gender relations underscored its achievement largely through cultural ascendancy—discursive persuasion—encouraging all to consent to, coalesce around, and routinely embody such unequal gender relations between men and women, between masculinity and femininity, and among masculinities.

For Connell, then, gender relations are seen as structured through inequality, injustice, and harm, and accordingly, the concepts of hegemonic masculinity and emphasized femininity are essential to Connell's framework, underlining how this feminized form works in tandem with hegemonic masculinity to legitimate masculine superordination and feminine subordination. But Connell recognized additional femininities both before and after the publication of *Gender and Power* (see Connell 1985a, 2007, 2012, 2014). In *Gender and Power*, Connell (1987, 183–84) argues that varieties of nonemphasized femininities are defined "by strategies of resistance or forms of noncompliance" as well as "by complex strategic combinations of compliance, resistance and co-operation." In short, emphasized femininity is a *specific* configuration of femininity that works to distinctly facilitate, in relation to hegemonic masculinity, the legitimation of gender hegemony. Thus, it is the routinely practiced unequal relationship that is crucial to the continuation of gender inequality within structured gender regimes.

Responding to the criticism that both radical and socialist feminism disregard agency, Connell included throughout *Gender and Power* a strong emphasis on the agency of the subject in the formation of gender.[7] Connell's theory of practice concentrates on what individuals *do* to constitute the social relations in which they live, and necessarily involves the interweaving of personal life and social structure. Connell (1987, 94, emphasis added) theorizes the "active presence of structure *in* practice" and the "active constitution of structure *by* practice." For example, Connell discusses the matrifocal family structure of a working-class community in Bethnal Green, London, in which the mother is the core figure and mother-daughter relations are the axis of the family. During daily interaction, "[d]aughters and mothers pop in and out of each other's houses up to twelve times a day; they exchange services like care in sickness and negotiate about family relationships—including the daughter's marriage" (93). Here, the structural relationship between mothers and daughters is constituted and reconstituted through active social practices and interactional rituals, and Connell uses this example to illustrate the ways that social structure is embodied in the everyday practices of—in this case— mothers and daughters.

Beyond this, Connell argues that gender practices are creative and inventive, yet these capacities are structured by particular social situations defined through structured gender relations. In gender practice, "there is a strong sense of the constraining power of gender relations (and other structures like class and race), a sense of something that people fetch up against" (Connell 1987, 61). Nevertheless, because "human action involves free invention" and "human knowledge is reflexive," Connell argues that "practice can be turned against what constrains it; so, structure can be deliberately the object of practice" (95). Although practice cannot escape structure, Connell emphasizes that gender practices are never fully determined by structure because such practices involve the process of constructing oneself through agentic choices that can transcend given circumstances: "Humans project themselves into their future by their choices, by the way they negate and transcend the circumstances that are given to them to start with. The person is constructed as a 'project' of realizing oneself in a particular way" (211). For Connell (2002, 4), "people construct themselves as masculine or feminine." Connell points out that we practice gender willingly and often enjoy participating in constructing a particular gender identity:

> Wearing leather jacket and engineer boots, my body declares: I am pleased to be masculine; I cultivate toughness, hard edges, and assertiveness. Wearing lace collar and ruffled skirt, my body declares: I am pleased to be feminine; I cultivate softness, smooth and rounded forms, receptiveness. (Connell 2002, 4–5)

In other words, Connell makes clear that gender relations are sources of inequality, injustice, and harm (that we mentioned previously) but simultaneously sources of pleasure, enjoyment, satisfaction, recognition, and identity. Indeed, practicing specific gender identities sustains the relations between them and, consequently, may support gender inequality, injustice, and harm (5).

Connell argues that the orchestration of masculinities and femininities involves a process of "configuring" gender practices that are historical and, as such, always subject to change. And for Connell, recognizing masculinity and femininity as historical requires locating them firmly in the realm of social agency. The relationship between masculinity and femininity is always already a historical and situational phenomenon. As such, no uniform strategy of this relationship prevails throughout history. As Connell (1987, 186) writes in *Gender and Power* with regard to femininity, all feminine practices are historical and consequently as "relationships change, new forms of femininity emerge, and others disappear." Specifically regarding emphasized femininity, Connell (187, emphasis added) affirms that the form of emphasized femininity "given most cultural and ideological support *at present*" (meaning, she wrote this more than thirty years ago) involved, for example, "the display of sociability rather than technical competence, fragility in mating scenes, compliance with men's desire for titillation and ego stroking . . . acceptance of marriage and childcare." This *form* of emphasized femininity is distinct to a particular time and place, not universal throughout history. Yet, emphasized femininity as a configuration of gender practice more generally is not a historical artifact. Rather, like hegemonic masculinity, the composition of emphasized femininity is ever changing, yet in different time periods this particular configuration of femininity always already operates in ways that legitimate gender hegemony.

Finally, Connell's perspective has always been about more than gender—in particular, the interplay between class and gender is prevalent throughout *Gender and Power*. Consider just one example of how Connell demonstrates diversity in emphasized femininities while moving gender analysis beyond the socialist feminist concentration on the *interaction* of class and gender and toward examinations of how class and gender *mutually constitute*, and thus form and transform, each other. In *Gender and Power*, Connell (1987, 266–67) discusses the patriarchal nature of the heterosexual working-class Markham family, noting that Mrs. Markham is "the hub" of family discussions and decisions and the source of strength for others. She also is conscious of gender inequality because her mother could see no point in her attending college to become a journalist, and consequently, Mrs. Markham has alternatively chosen to become a working-class homemaker. Pushed by Mrs. Markham to do well in school, the oldest daughter in the family is an "A" student and is likewise aware of gender inequality but struggles with the working-class nature of schooling. She often comes home from school in tears, a sadness that develops out of tension and frustration from experiencing school as a "dead" place—she therefore seriously considers leaving school despite her academic success.

Mr. Markham works in a warehouse and earns below average wages; he gets pushed around at work, and the work situation offends his pride in workmanship and erodes his masculine self-esteem. He attempted to maintain a hegemonic masculinity-emphasized femininity relationship with his wife, but the result was that he became increasingly marginalized in the household. His wife and daughter have concluded that he has failed as a husband and father, and he accepts this opinion of himself.

Connell uses this account and brief description to demonstrate the ongoing constitution of class and gender relations through practice within the Markham family and how that reciprocity accounts for the problems that arise, such as where women fit into the world, access to resources for girls, the division of household labor, the authority of men, the character of masculinity and femininity, the nature of working-class schooling and its impact on girls, and the meanings of hegemonic masculinity and emphasized femininity (Connell 1987, 267). Mrs. Markham, Mr. Markham, and their daughter find themselves positioned in discrete ways within their common working-class environment. To be working class implies something different for all three, which is constituted in their varying gender constructions and relations. Despite these differences, the three participants in this setting mutually establish a unique form of working-class gender hegemony. And the specific agentic sexual politics of Mrs. Markham and her daughter were completely developed out of their combined class and gender experiences, as neither had contact with the feminist movement of the time.

There are many groundbreaking aspects of Connell's *Gender and Power*— it became, and remains, an exceptionally significant contribution to feminist sociology. But for our purposes here, Connell was unique for recognizing the significance of both *choice* and *routine* to gender practice. Connell's work was pioneering in our conception of gender practice in the sense that she theorized gender relations in such a way that it was possible to understand people as agentic actors, capable of constructing gendered identities in part through agentic choices that transcend given circumstances. And Connell emphasizes that, in each particular "gender regime," there exists routine ways gender is practiced and configured, such as hegemonic masculinity and emphasized femininity, whose recurring and relational embodiment of unequal gender identities is crucial to the continuation of structured gender hegemony. Nevertheless, neither choice nor routine are analyzed and developed in detail by Connell. Accordingly, many readers of her theory have missed the significance of both choice and routine to gender practice and how they invariably are symbiotically connected.

Candace West and Don Zimmerman

During the same year that *Gender and Power* was published, Candace West and Don Zimmerman (1987) published their extremely influential article "Doing Gender." In this article, West and Zimmerman distinguish "sex" (one's birth classification), "sex category" (the social identification as a woman or a man), and "gender" (social action that validates sex and sex category). They argue that social actors attribute the "correct" sex to individuals when they display the "appropriate" social signs of a sex category. For

West and Zimmerman, individuals attempt to adorn themselves in culturally appropriate gendered signifiers, and daily, in every interaction, they engage in gender attribution—people identify and categorize copresent interactants into sex categories while they simultaneously categorize themselves for others.

Nevertheless, "doing gender" means more than simply "required iden-tificatory displays" and gender attribution, and thus the social signs of sex category (West and Zimmerman 1987, 127). Rather, according to West and Zimmerman, it involves a "situated accomplishment," or "the activity of managing situated conduct in light of normative conceptions, attitudes, and activities appropriate to one's sex category" (127). While sex category refers to social identification as a woman or man, gender is the processual corroboration of that identification and is accomplished in social interaction; individuals coordinate their activities to "do" gender in situational ways. As West and Zimmerman (126) make clear, "doing gender" entails "a routine, methodical and recurring accomplishment."

Crucial to their conceptualization of gender as a situated yet routine accomplishment is the notion of "accountability." For West and Zimmerman (1987, 137), "to 'do' gender is not always to live up to normative concep-tions of femininity and masculinity; it is to engage in behavior *at the risk of assessment.*" The risk of assessment is what compels individuals to "do" gender because when people realize their behavior may be assessed and held accountable by others, they construct their social actions in relation to how they might be interpreted in the particular social contexts in which they occur. Since sex category is always pertinent, an individual involved in essentially any social practice may be held accountable for the accomplishment of that practice in gendered ways.

Moreover, according to West and Zimmerman (1987), individuals expect others to attribute a particular sex category to them—a sex category that cor-responds to their "essential nature"—and people satisfy the ongoing task of accountability by interactionally encouraging sex categorizations by means of concocted behaviors that may be interpreted accordingly. Individuals configure their practices such that they are seen unquestionably by others in particular social situations as expressing their sex category, and thus, they "do" masculinity or femininity to qualify that sex category. In other words, "doing gender" involves the situated management of conduct by sex-categorized individuals held accountable to situational perceptions of acceptable gendered practices. In this view, then, masculinity and femininity are *accomplished* in and through interaction; they are not something done to men and women or something settled beforehand. And masculinity and femi-ninity are never static, never a finished product. Rather, people "do" gender in particular ways in specific social situations, although not in circumstances of their own choosing.

Like Connell's theory, West and Zimmerman's conception of "doing gender" became, and remains, immensely salient in feminist sociology. There is much more to say about this theory, but for our purposes here, West and Zimmerman recognize gender as a "routine, methodical, and recurring accomplishment" (126). This implies that "doing gender" is done according to continuously (re)established procedures—it is methodical and thus, habitual. And "doing gender" also entails, according to West and Zimmerman, "managing situated conduct," meaning individuals consciously preside over, govern, and bring about specific behavior, thus exhibiting forms of deliberations and agency in the formulation of gender practices. The notion that individuals additionally realize their behavior may be assessed, likewise, strongly suggests the existence of conscious decisions on the part of social actors in producing a particular favorable, and thus accountable, result. Nevertheless, and again like Connell, neither agency nor routine is analyzed and developed in detail by West and Zimmerman. Not surprisingly, then, many miss the significance of both to "doing gender," their dynamic relationship, and how they may be symbiotically connected. In short, agency and routine are insufficiently theorized by West and Zimmerman, as well as by other scholars who apply this theory.

PRIORITIZING GENDER PRACTICE AS EXCLUSIVELY REFLEXIVE OR ROUTINE

Since the publication of Connell's book *Gender and Power* and West and Zimmerman's "Doing Gender" article, a few feminist sociologists of gender became interested in scrutinizing reflexive and routine gender practices, but they did so by continuing to uncouple reflexivity and routine and, thus, theoretically prioritized gender practice as either *exclusively* reflexive or routine. In this section we present two such examples.

James W. Messerschmidt

Messerschmidt (2012, 2016, 2018b) utilized life-history interviews to examine how reflexivity and gendered identity intersect in the development of teenage boys and girls. Messerschmidt acknowledged that teenagers sometimes engage in unreflexive routine gendered social action. Their gendered practices were accomplished according to situational criteria, yet they occasionally did not intend their practices specifically as gendered acts. Using West and Zimmerman's (1987) language, accountability encouraged them to act in certain unreflexive gendered ways within particular social contexts. Messerschmidt, however, prioritized social action as exclusively reflexive because, in his research on youth involved in assaultive and sexual violence, he found that in this type of behavior, reflexivity plays a significant role in both masculine and feminine practices—especially in the social context of bullying.

Methodologically, life-history interviews demonstrate gendered identities as trajectories through time, as patterns of reflexive agency. The boys' and girls' reflexivity mediated their particular social experiences at school, and their subjective deliberation is essential to understanding their decisions to engage in violence/nonviolence to solve various gendered dilemmas. The life-history interviews recorded the particular social conditions that impacted each youth as well as the specific reflexive deliberations that mediated and negotiated those social conditions. For example, the life-history data documented how social conditions made each boy and girl feel, it uncovered what each youth reflexively defined as their immediate concern, and it revealed how each boy and girl planned and ultimately decided to engage in violence or nonviolence.

For Messerschmidt, the boys and girls were not free to make and remake their gendered selves however they chose. They were constrained (and enabled) by the particular social conditions situationally available to them. What can futher be gleaned from their life stories is the insight that teenagers reflexively reproduce gender inequality and the accompanying gender identities when they practice complicity with the in-school dominant masculinities and femininities. Nevertheless, Messerschmidt concluded that, for both boys and girls, gender practice was exclusively reflexive, missing the coexistence of reflexivity and routine in gender practice and identity formation.

Matthew Desmond

In his ethnographic analysis of wildland firefighters, Matthew Desmond (2006) makes the opposite argument: gender practice is prioritized as exclusively routine rather than reflexive. Desmond asked why certain individuals seek high-risk occupations when safer ways of earning a living are available. That is, why do working-class "country boys" become wildland firefighters, and how, in the process, do they construct durable masculine identities? According to Desmond (2006), through socialization within working-class family life, young boys who grow up in rural settings and eventually become wildland firefighters acquire a "country-masculine *habitus*." This form of *habitus* (Bourdieu 1984), and an associated gender identity, involves a certain way of dressing, consuming, speaking, and eating, as well as routine social practices that differentiate "country boys" from others. These working-class boys carry this country-masculine *habitus* and identity with them to the US Forest Service for employment as wildland firefighters. Desmond traces what

Bourdieu ([1997] 2000) refers to as the *general habitus* of self-described country boys and shows how it becomes socially embodied in ways that produce little friction as it transforms into the *specific habitus* required of wildland firefighters. As Desmond points out, by embodying a country-masculine *habitus*, working-class country boys come to know that

> the kind of men who fight wildfire are the kind of men their fathers are, the kind of men they are, or at least the kind of men they want to be. They belong . . . and feel at home here because they concur, mind, body and soul, with a firmly established corporate sense regarding the beliefs and practices that make up a country-masculine lifestyle. (2006, 396)

Working-class country boys become wildland firefighters for the money and masculine adventure, but especially for "the *esprit de corps* that comes with a collectively shared lifestyle" (Desmond 2006, 397). And this masculine know-how compels them to quickly "adapt to the challenges of the fire" (407). In addition to acquiring knowledge about how to "dig line, back burn, fall dead trees (snags), recognize fire behavior, and interpret weather patterns," the new wildland firefighter-masculine *habitus* involves learning how to communicate and think like other wildland firefighters, all of which aligns well with the country-masculine *habitus* (405).

For Desmond (2006, 411), then, country boys easily gravitate toward wildland firefighting "because the country-masculine *habitus* seeks out a universe in which it can recognize itself, an environment in which it can thrive." There is, according to Desmond, an elective affinity between the *general habitus* they acquire growing up as country boys and the *specific habitus* required in wildland firefighting. As Desmond puts it, the decision to become a wildland firefighter is "not a bold leap into a brave new world, but rather, a mild step into familiar territory" (411). Country boys happily embrace the high-risk work of wildland firefighting and, thus, for the most part reproduce the masculine *habitus* embodied at home.

In Desmond's work, it is reflexivity that goes unrecognized as well as any conception of how interaction and social conditions impact country boys. For Desmond, individual country boys embody a particular masculine *habitus*, which in turn is easily and routinely adaptable to a new social situation. Desmond's emphasis is on the smooth reproduction of a routine and similar masculine identity within two different contexts. And this is in line with Bourdieu's perspective, as he often emphasized that dispositions are transposable between similar but not identical contexts, and thus, routine social reproduction takes place. Desmond thus prioritizes gender practice as exclusively routine and thus does not address the significance of reflexivity and its relationship with routine in the country-boys' and the wildland firefighters' gender practices and identities.

GENDER, REFLEXIVITY, AND THE *HABITUS*

Most sociologists of gender who focus on routine gendered practices, like Desmond, turn to Bourdieu's (1984) theorization of routine as practices that are not only unreflexive but also beyond the bounds of reflexivity. Bourdieu argues that the *habitus* is produced through dispositions embedded in the unconscious that compel people to act in ways that routinely reproduce identities that achieve durability through context, routine, and repetition. For Bourdieu, the *habitus* constitutes collections of stable dispositions, and thus routine identities that are also capable of adaptation and transformation as they move through social life. Individuals adjust to diverse social situations without consciously (and thus reflexively) considering each adjustment as it is being made. Bourdieu is therefore explicitly mechanical and deterministic in his conceptualization of the *habitus*.[8] For example, he suggests that the effect of the *habitus* is the creation of "agents who are equipped with *and will* behave in a certain way in certain circumstances" (Bourdieu 1990, 77, emphasis added), and that the embodied *habitus* "is placed beyond the grasp of consciousness and hence cannot be touched by voluntary, deliberate transformation, cannot even be made explicit" (Bourdieu 1977, 94). For Bourdieu (1998, 54–55), then, social practices and thus identities are conceptualized as caused by "deeply buried corporeal dispositions, outside the channels of consciousness and calculation." Reflexivity only emerges in Bourdieu's calculation when the compatibility between *habitus* and social context is disrupted; strategic thought and conscious deliberation occur solely in conditions of rupture or "crisis" within Bourdieu's framework. And ultimately, the *habitus* guides that awakened conscious reflexivity. For Bourdieu, routine trumps reflexivity.

Although Bourdieu does consider both routine and reflexivity—while emphasizing and prioritizing the former—his theory has been subjected to critique. For example, Margaret Archer (2013, 7) points out that it is hard to see "how routine principles of action, adjusted to a very different earlier setting, can supply appropriate guidelines for acting once that context has been 'brutally' displaced." Our conception of routine—which centers on a sociological analysis rather than invoking the unconscious (see "Theory and Methods")—builds on this critique, demonstrating that the notion of *habitus* misses important social processes in the production of gendered practice. Burawoy (2012) agrees, arguing that the *habitus* is both unknowable and unverifiable:

> Bourdieu never gives us the tools to examine what an individual's habitus might be. It's a black box. We infer the habitus from behavior—a shop lifter is a shop lifter because she has the habitus of a shoplifter. We only know the habitus from its effects; there's no theory of its components or how they are formed. . . . In short, habitus is not a scientific concept but a folk concept with a fancy name—a concept without content. (204)

Analytically, the *habitus* cannot exist if reflexivity is present because, for Bourdieu, the latter contradicts the former. Bourdieu fails to explain the sociological processes through which unconscious embodied dispositions mutate into consciousness and calculation within specific "crisis" situations. Indeed, in this way, Bourdieu's theory of the *habitus* can be productively understood as teleological. As we argue throughout this book, reflexivity can and does exist in dramatic fashion, even in the absence of crises, and routine gendered practices can properly be understood sociologically rather than deferring to the unconscious.

Despite criticisms of Bourdieu's notion of *habitus*, some feminist sociologists have conceptualized reflexivity and routine in new ways by challenging Bourdieu, while others continue to work within Bourdieu's framework by coupling reflexivity with *habitus*. We discuss the former first through the example of an engaging article by Lisa Adkins.

Lisa Adkins

Adkins (2004) disagrees with Bourdieu and argues that reflexivity does not exclusively emerge under "crisis" situations or movement across overlapping contexts. Instead, Adkins (203) maintains that reflexivity is "increasingly characteristic of gender" today and has, in fact, become routine. She reviews studies of gender in the workplace, recording that workplace practices encourage reflexivity which in turn muddles characteristics traditionally associated with masculinity and femininity. As Adkins (202) writes, "for both men and women, gender is increasingly taking the form of a self-conscious artifice which can be managed, strategically deployed and performed." Adkins shows the fluidity of gender including how gender practices are reflexively constructed for audiences in different contexts. For example, in one of the studies reviewed by Adkins, a financial service worker (203) is quoted as stating that her particular constructions of gender depend upon whom she is interacting with: sometimes she will choose "the executive bimbo look" while at other times she will wear a "very smart tailored blue dress" that "looks tremendously, you know, professional." In other words, this financial service worker reflexively chose to construct femininity in different ways, depending upon the context.

Adkins concludes that gender reflexivity is becoming increasingly routine in modern societies resulting in a constant reworking of gender practice and identity. Such a development suggests that "the Bourdieusian influenced accounts of transformations in gender" fail "to register that reflexivity does not concern liberal freedom from gender but may be tied to new arrangements of gender" (Adkins 2004, 203). Thus, for Adkins (2004), Bourdieu's model of reflexivity underestimates the extent to which reflexivity is part and parcel of everyday life. Not only is gender reflexivity exhibited in contexts devoid of the crises Bourdieu proposed, but reflexivity is so common for Adkins that it is productively understood as routine itself.

We agree with Adkins's claim that gender practices and identity formation often result from reflexivity, but this does not entail that gender practice is in effect exclusively reflexive. Given that everyone engages in both gender reflexivity and gender routine, it is important to empirically investigate when gender reflexivity and gender routine occur in everyday life, and when and how they are interconnected, symbiotically related, and thus develop through a mutually beneficial relationship within gender practices and identity formations. We now turn our attention to Barbara Risman's theory of "gender as social structure."

Barbara Risman

Risman (2018a, 2018b) conceptualizes gender as a social structure, a stratification system involving three levels of analysis: individual (the formation of different gender identities), interaction (gender stability and change depending upon interactional expectations), and macro (how gender is embedded in institutions and organizations). Risman's perspective highlights, at each level and across levels, both the recursive relationship between cultural and material processes and how structure shapes choice and interaction while human agency creates, sustains, and modifies structure.

For our purposes here, Risman argues that individual gender identities are constructed through interaction with others, and such interactions occur within institutional and organizational settings. Risman acknowledges the importance of both gender reflexivity and gender routine to identity formation, conceptualizing the former as occurring when individuals consciously interpret their own lives and social practices. Risman asserts that often people engage in gendered social action for their own reasons and that it is essential to document agentic choice when researching gender behavior. Risman writes:

> When people act on structure, they do so for their own reasons. We must, there-
> fore, be concerned with why actors choose their acts. Actions alter the world
> we have entered; institutions are powerful but not determinative. (2018b, 31)

Beyond reflexivity, Risman follows Bourdieu by identifying gender routine as habituated cultural knowledge that becomes an unconscious internalized aspect of one's gendered self. According to Risman (2018b, 32), "Actors often behave without thinking about it, simply following habits that come to define the cultural meaning of their lives." Risman relies on Bourdieu's notion of *habitus* in conceptualizing gender routine because it is the *habitus* that allegedly gives rise to the possibility of how gendered social actions become habitually practiced: "The habitus generates the possibility of what actions can be imagined. While some people clearly do reject childhood train-ing, they cannot do it outside the boundaries of their *habitus*, beyond their imagination" (35). Notwithstanding, Risman (2018a, 35) uniquely recognizes the significance of both routine—albeit as *habitus*—and reflexivity by argu-ing that, because of the former, "actors often behave without thinking about it," and regarding the latter, "human beings reflexively monitor the intended and unintended consequences of their actions."

Like the perspectives by Connell and West and Zimmerman, Risman's theory has been highly influential in feminist sociology. Although there are additional aspects of her theory that could be discussed, for our purposes here, it is notable and unusual that Risman considers both gender reflexivity and gender routine as part of gender practice and identity formation. Even though she does not elaborate, Risman registers that there exists a "reflexive monitoring" connection between reflexivity *and* routine. This recognition by Risman advances feminist sociological theory by pointing to a link between reflexivity and routine. In this book we build on this insight by closely exam-ining the where, when, and how of such monitoring. Risman's perspective, however, embraces a contested concept—the *habitus*. In contrast, we con-ceptualize the link between reflexivity and routine by pursuing a thoroughly *sociological* comprehension of routine, as well as elucidating in detail the symbiotic interconnections between reflexivity and routine.

In this book, we elaborate on and add detail to the foregoing body of theory and scholarship, conceptualizing reflexivity and routine as symbiotically entangled, and arguing that it is their coexistence and interplay that shape sex, gender, and sexual practices and identities. Our perspective ("Theory and Methods") documents and signals *how* both reflexivity and routine have a more interdependent relationship than has been previously theorized. And rather than interrogating sex, gender, and sexual practice as *either* routine *or* reflexive, or routine as developed through an unconscious *habitus*, we present data from two life-history interviews ("Identity Reminiscences") that document routine as a conscious—albeit unreflexive—sex, gender, and sexual practice, and both routine and reflexive sex, gender, and sexual practices as typical and extensive rather than exceptional. The two interviewees—both of whom eventually identified as genderqueer—constructed a kaleidoscope of sex, gender, and sexual identities through a symbiotic nexus between routine and reflexive practices (conditioned by context) that provides a useful illustration of our theoretical perspective. Arguably, contemporary theoretical tools in the sociology of gender overlook an understanding of the dynamic interplay between reflexivity and routine in sex, gender, and sexual practices and identity formations. To remedy this, our perspective demonstrates reflexivity and routine in a more symbiotic association than is often assumed. Without prioritizing either, we explore this relationship by examining the ways reflexivity and routine collaboratively shape sex, gender, and sexual identities and practices over the course of the two interviewees' lives. In "Theory and Method", we outline this framework for conceptualizing the symbiotic connection between reflexive and routine practices.

NOTES

1. Importantly, modern uses of "gender" popular today were less common then. If gender was used to refer to a distinction between men and women, for instance, it would have been used in ways roughly synonymous with "sex." Dating the origins of modern uses of "gender" is difficult. But two early uses of "gender" (as distinguished explicitly from "sex") are British feminist sociologist Ann Oakley's (1972) *Sex, Gender, and Society* (about which we write more later) and the psychologist Robert Stoller's (1968) *Sex and Gender: On the Development of Masculinity and Femininity.* For this reason, early feminist work theorizing gender often utilizes language that might seem strange by modern standards, like the anthropologist Margaret Mead's (1935) work examining differences in three separate societies' understanding of gender where she refers to gender as "sex temperament," or Erving Goffman's (1968) reference to gender differences as between "sex classes." "Gender," as it is used and theorized today, emerged sometime in the late 1960s and early 1970s and did not catch on immediately.

2. It is worth noting that there is a kind of biological reductionism at play in Millet's work that was also present in the reigning sociological theory making sense of gender at the time: sex role theory. At times in Millet's work, she writes about "women" and "men," but these are used interchangeably throughout her work with "females" and "males." Raewyn Connell (1985a, 1987) points out a similar issue at work in the conceptualization of sex role theory, which she also presents as biologically reductionistic (for different reasons and in different ways) in that the theory itself awkwardly paired a *biological* classification ("sex") with a sociological one ("role").

3. Jeffrey Weeks (1986) refers to this penchant to attribute biological explanations to things we are unable to explain another way even in the absence of biological evidence that such explanations are accurate as subscribing to what he refers to as the "black hole hypothesis." Because of the cultural prestige of biological sciences, explanations attributed to biology are sometimes presented as more legitimate. But this can also lead to a "black hole," wherein when no satisfactory social and cultural explanation has been provided for a behavior, practice, or phenomenon, cultural biases toward biological explanations sometimes situate biologically deterministic explanations as supported simply by an absence of other evidence supporting alternative explanations for any particular phenomenon.

4. Initial critiques of the earliest theory of gender in sociology (the structural functionalist sex role theory) are an illustration of this shift as those early critiques centered on sex role theory's inability not only to address power and inequality but also to acknowledge agency. The perspective was both biologically foundationalist and structurally deterministic (see Stacey and Thorne 1985 and Connell 1985a).

5. Connell only referred to these separate systems of relations as "substructures" once in *Gender and Power*: "[T]he concept of a single structure of gender relations must be broken down into component structures or substructures" (1987, 91). Later, in a less cited article, "Encounters with Structure" (2004), Connell again relies on this language to examine the ways such interlocking systems of relations can be best understood in her theory of gender as "a structure of social relations" (19).

6. This concept in Connell's theory of gender relations was actually borrowed from Jill Matthews's *Good and Mad Women: The Historical Construction of Femininity in Twentieth-Century Australia* (1984), where Matthews deployed the concept to describe historically emergent and constructed patterns of both power relations between women and men as well as social and cultural definitions of femininity and masculinity. Connell borrowed the concept to represent a "structural inventory for an entire society" (1987, 99).

7. Indeed, a major critique of structural functionalism more generally (and sex role theory specifically as it pertains to this work) was that the theoretical model was, like radical and socialist feminism, ultimately structurally deterministic. The theory relied on a belief in a kind of universal voluntarism on the part of social actors to explain why everyone would take on gendered social roles. Additionally, however, by ignoring gender "deviance," it failed to account for evidence of agency (see Connell 1985a). In attempting to produce a more thoroughly sociological framework for understanding gender, Connell was explicitly concerned with accounting for agency, deviance, and the possibility that gendered change might emerge both from structural shifts in society as well as in more localized transformations in gender relations themselves.

8. "*Habitus*" is untranslated from the original language in which Bourdieu's work was published—French. It has been defined and described in different ways. One definition that is helpful is his occasional usage of "*le sens practique*," which loosely translates as "the practical sense," but some have suggested that "a feel for the game" is a comparable translation as well.

Theory and Method

In "Theory and Method," we present a new theoretical framework—what we label "structured action theory"—for conceptualizing not simply gender but also sex, gender, and sexual practices and identities. To understand the social construction of sex, gender, and sexuality, we must first grasp what has been understood as "doing" sex, gender, and sexuality. Following this, we discuss how the theory conceptualizes sex, gender, and sexuality in relation to the symbiotic link between reflexivity and routine; reflexive and routine embodiment; structured action; sex, gender, and sexual hegemony; and non-hegemonic subordinate sexes, genders, and sexualities. We close "Theory and Method" with a brief discussion of the methodology of the study from which the two life stories outlined in "Identity Reminiscences" are drawn.

STRUCTURED ACTION THEORY

To grasp the relationship among and the social construction of sex, gender, and sexual practices and identities, we now outline structured action theory. We begin with a discussion of how this theory incorporates and builds on the framework of "doing gender" first theorized by West and Zimmerman (1987).

Doing and Determining Sex, Gender, and Sexuality

Building on various theoretical origins (Archer 2003, 2007, 2012; Connell 1987, 1995; Giddens 1976, 1984; Goffman 1963, 1972, 1979; Kessler and McKenna 1978; Risman 2004, 2018a, 2018b; Sartre 1956; West and Fenstermaker 1995; West and Zimmerman 1987), structured action theory emphasizes the reflexive and routine construction of sex, gender, and sexuality as situated social, interactional, and embodied accomplishments. In other words, sex, gender, and sexuality are all social constructions and grow out of embodied social practices in specific social structural settings and serve to inform such practices in reciprocal relation. Understanding each is essential to conceptualizing various formations of sex, gender, and sexual identities.

Regarding *sex*, historical and social conditions shape the character and definition of "sex" (e.g., social identification or classification as "male" or "female"). Sex identities and their meanings are given concrete expression by the specific social relations and historical context within which they are embedded. Historical studies on sex classification and categorization show its clear association with sexuality, and gender has been shown to be always already involved.

The work of Thomas Laqueur (1990) is exemplary in this regard. In his important book *Making Sex*, Laqueur shows that for 2,000 years a "one-sex model" dominated scientific and popular thought in which male and female bodies were not conceptualized in terms of difference. From antiquity to the beginning of the seventeenth century, male and female bodies were seen as having the same body parts, even in terms of genitalia, with the vagina regarded as an interior penis, the vulva as foreskin, the uterus as scrotum, and the ovaries as testicles. Women were understood as having the same body as men, but the positioning of its parts was different. As one doggerel verse of the period stated, "women are but men turned outside in" (Laqueur 1990, 4). In the "one-sex model," the sexes were not seen as different in *kind* but rather in *degree*—woman was understood as a lesser form of man. And as Laqueur explains, "*Sex*, or the body, must be understood as the epiphenomenon, while *gender*, what we would take to be a cultural category, was primary or 'real'" (8). Inequality was imposed on bodies from the outside and seen as God's "marker" of a male and female distinction. To be a man or a woman was to have a specific place in society decreed by God. Describing the worldview that shaped the one-sex model, Lacqueur writes, "Anatomy in the context of sexual difference was a representational strategy that illuminated a more stable extracorporeal reality. There existed many genders, but only one adaptable sex" (35). Lacqueur discovered, in other words, that "sex before the seventeenth century . . . was still a sociological and not an ontological category" (8).

Laqueur argues that after the Enlightenment a "two-sex model" involving a foundational dichotomy between now two (and only two) discrete and opposite sexes emerged. No longer did scientific and popular thought "regard woman as a lesser version of man along a vertical axis of infinite gradations but rather an altogether different creature along a horizontal axis whose middle ground was largely empty" (Laqueur 1990, 148). And Foucault's (1980, vii) well-known discussion of the "hermaphrodite" *Herculine Barbin* (a group referred to today as people with intersex traits) demonstrates that by the mid-1800s there was no allowance for any human being to occupy a "middle ground" through "a mixture of two sexes in a single body," which consequently limited "the free choice of indeterminate individuals," and thus henceforth "everybody was to have one and only one sex." Individuals accepted previously as representatives of the "middle ground" (i.e., individuals with intersex traits) were now required to submit to expert medical diagnosis to uncover their "true" sex.[1] Foucault continues:

> Everybody was to have his or her primary, profound, determined and determining sexual identity; as for the elements of the other sex that might appear, they could only be accidental, superficial, or even quite simply illusory. From the medical point of view, this meant that when confronted with a hermaphrodite, the doctor was no longer concerned with recognizing the presence of the two sexes, juxtaposed or intermingled, or with knowing which of the two prevailed over the other, but rather with deciphering the true sex that was hidden beneath ambiguous appearances. (1980, vii)

Arguably, then, within the "two-sex model" it became commonplace to view *the* male sex and *the* female sex as "different in every conceivable aspect of body and soul, in every physical and moral aspect—An anatomy and physiology of incommensurability replaced a metaphysics of hierarchy in the representation of woman in relation to man" (Laqueur 1990, 5–6).

Perhaps predictably, these two now fixed, incommensurable, opposite sexes also are conceptualized as *the* source of the political, economic, and cultural lives of men and women (gender and sexuality), since "biology—the stable, ahistorical, sexed body—is understood to be the epistemic foundation for prescriptive claims about the social order" (Laqueur 1990, 6). For instance, passivity, submissiveness, and vulnerability were now understood as "natural" aspects of women's gender, just as activity, aggression, and invulnerability were understood as "inherent" aspects of men's gender. And given that anatomy was newly understood as destiny, a heterosexual instinct to procreate was only now understood to proceed from the body as "the natural state of the architecture of two incommensurable opposite sexes" (233).

The shift in thinking to a "two-sex model," consisting now of two different types of humans with complementary heterosexual natures and desires, corresponded with the emergence of the public/private split: It was now "natural" for men to enter the public realm of society and for women to remain in the private sphere. Explaining these distinctly gendered social spaces was "resolved by grounding social and cultural differentiation of the sexes in a biology of incommensurability" (Laqueur 1990, 19). In other words, "gender" and "sexuality" became subordinated to "sex," and biology became primary: *the* foundation of difference and inequality between men and women.

Laqueur makes clear that the transition to a two-sex model was *ideological*, not scientific; the reevaluation of the body as primary occurred approximately 100 years before supporting scientific discoveries appeared. And although anatomical and physiological differences clearly exist between male and female bodies, what counts as "sex" is determined socially. In short, natural scientists had no interest in "seeing" two distinct sexes at the anatomical and concrete physiological level "until such differences became politically important," and "sex" therefore became "explicable only within the context of battles over gender and power" (Laqueur 1990, 10, 11). From this perspective, the two-sex model can be understood as a kind of biological fiction with a political function.

The historical work of both Laqueur and Foucault suggests that "sex differences" do not naturally precede "gender and sexual differences." And as Wendy Cealey Harrison (2006) insightfully observes, it is virtually impossible to ever entirely separate the body and our understanding of it from its socially determined milieu. Arguably, what is now necessary is a reconceptualization of "the taken-for-grantedness of 'sex' as a form of categorization for human beings and examining the ways in which such a categorization is built" (Cealey Harrison 2006, 43).

Following this suggestion by Cealey Harrison, it is important to recognize that in an important early work from the 1970s, Suzanne Kessler and Wendy McKenna (1978) argue that social action is constructed through taken-for-granted discourses, or what they call "incorrigible propositions."[2] Our belief in two objectively real, biologically created constant yet opposite sexes is a telling discourse. We assume there are only two sexes; each person is simply an example of one or the other. In other words, we construct a sex binary in which no binary holds biologically, historically, cross-culturally, and contemporaneously (Messerschmidt 2004).

The key process in the social construction of the sex binary is the active way we decide what sex a person is (Kessler and McKenna 1978, 1–20). Kessler and McKenna show through a series of ethnomethodological studies that a significant part of this sex attribution process is the notion that men have penises and women do not.[3] We consider genitals the ultimate criterion in constructing sex assignments; yet, in our daily interactions we continually occasion sex attributions with a complete lack of information about others' genitals. Our recognition of another's sex is dependent upon the exhibit of such bodily characteristics as speech, hair, clothing, physical appearance, and other aspects of personal front—through this embodied presentation we are "doing" *sex*, and it is this doing that becomes a substitute for the concealed genitalia. In short, "sex" and consequently sex identity is socially constructed. As Kessler and McKenna (1978, 18) put it, "The gender attribution process is the method by which we construct our world of two genders."

Nevertheless, "doing" *gender* (West and Zimmerman 1987), and thus qualifying *sex*, entails considerably more than the "social emblems" representing membership in one of two sex categories. Rather, the social construction of gender practice involves situated social, interactional, and embodied accomplishments. Gender grows out of social practice in specific settings that concurrently inform such practices in reciprocal relation. Although "sex" defines social identification as "male" or "female," "doing gender" systematically corroborates and qualifies that sex category and identity through embodied social interaction. In effect, gender is constituted through a plurality of forms but takes shape *within interactions* themselves. Societal members coordinate social practice to accomplish gender in situationally "appropriate" ways (West and Zimmerman 1987), with gender (and thus "sex") "determined" in different institutional and cultural contexts (e.g., Meadow 2010; Pfeffer 2014; Westbrook and Schilt 2014; Nisar 2017).[4] During most interactions, one's sex identity and gender identity are indistinguishable because society is organized around the expectation of their *congruence* within the same practices (Messerschmidt 2018a). This congruence, furthermore, is also socially and culturally enforced via social institutions and accountability structures.

Accordingly, early gender identity development in childhood occurs through an interactive process between and among children and adults. By reason of this interaction with others—and the social structures this interaction constitutes—children (for the most part) undertake to practice what is being preached, represented, and structured. Raewyn Connell defines the proactive adoption of specific embodied gender practices as the "moment of engagement," the moment when a person initiates an identity of masculinity or femininity as his or her own (1995, 122).[5] The young child has in effect located their self in relation to others within a sexed and gendered structured field (Jackson 2007). Children negotiate the socially structured sexed and gendered identities and their accompanying discourses that are prevalent and attributed as such in their particular milieu(s) and, in so doing, commit themselves to a routine practice of sex and gender self-attribution and thus identity (e.g., "I'm a boy" or "I'm a girl"). This binary routine identity as a boy or as a girl is the primary mode by which social actors initially choose to relate to the world and to express themselves in it and, thus, serves to simultaneously enable and constrain in the social construction of sex, gender, and sexuality.

What makes us human is the fact that we construct ourselves by making reflexive choices that transcend given circumstances and propel us into a future defined, in part, by the consequences of those choices (Connell 1987). Doing sex and gender—normally mutually constituted—is a routine process through which agents construct patterns of embodied presentation and practice that suggest a particular binary sex (male/female) and gender (masculine/feminine) identity in specific settings and, consequently, project themselves into a future where new situations are encountered, and subsequently new reflexive and routine practices are made. And following Connell (2002), we agree that people "do" sex and gender willingly and often enjoy and find pleasure in their particular binary or nonbinary identities. There often exists unity and coherence to one's routine sex and gender identities in the sense that most people tend to embody this particular sexed and gendered identity and, thus, sex and gender binaries over time and space.

Nevertheless, and although agents construct both reflexive and routine practices as both male or female, masculine or feminine, the actual accomplishment of sex and gender may vary substantially by situation, institution, and context (e.g., Bridges 2009; Westbrook and Schilt 2014). That is, sex and gender are renegotiated continuously through social interaction, and therefore, one's sexed and gendered identities may be fraught with contradictions and diversity in sex/gender strategies and practices. For example, agents may situationally construct specific routine gender identities (e.g., masculine, feminine, nonbinary) that contradict their bodily sex identity (e.g., female).

Sexuality involves all erotic and nonerotic aspects of social life and social being that relate to bodily attraction or intimate bodily contact between individuals, such as arousal, desire, practice, discourse, interaction, and relationship (see Jackson and Scott 2010). "Doing" sexuality encompasses the same interactional processes discussed earlier for "doing sex and gender" and, therefore, likewise involves children initially acquiring knowledge primarily about heterosexuality through structured interactions with children and adults. This initial process involves the acquisition of mostly nonerotic forms of heterosexual discursive knowledge, such as heterosexual marital relationships that suggest this is "where babies come from"; however, to adopt such rudimentary heterosexual discursive knowledge, "doing sex" must take primacy. As Stevi Jackson and Sue Scott (2010, 91–92) point out, "We recognize someone as male or female before we make assumptions about heterosexuality or homosexuality; we cannot logically do otherwise." The heterosexual/homosexual socially structured binary hinges on meaningful sex categories, "on being able to 'see' two men or two women as 'the same' and a man and a woman as 'different'" (92). The structured notion of two and only two sexes establishes discursively the rationale for the heterosexual/homosexual socially structured binary.

Once children begin to develop a sense of the erotic aspects of sexuality—which usually occurs through interaction with peers in secondary school—their sense-making is governed by embodied sexed and gendered identities (Jackson 2007). That is, our conceptualization of sex and gender impacts our understanding and practice of sexuality (both the erotic and the nonerotic aspects), and it is through sexual practices (once again both the erotic and the nonerotic) that we validate sex and gender. Agents adopt embodied sexual practices as a "moment of engagement," a moment when the individual begins to affix a specific routine sexual identity to their sexed and gendered identities, constructing, for example, heteromasculine and heterofeminine identities and understandings of the self. The accomplishment together of sex, gender, and sexual identities within the same practices mutually constitutes embodied individuals, and interaction with others is essential to one's ability to negotiate and fit in to ongoing and situationally structured patterns of sex, gender, and sexuality.

Crucial to this negotiation and "fitting in" is the notion of "accountability" (West and Zimmerman 1987; Hollander 2013, 2018). Accountability refers to individuals anticipating assessment of their behavior and configuring and orchestrating their embodied actions in relation to how such actions may be interpreted by others and by themselves in particular social contexts.[6] Accountability means presenting sex and gender identities that others can recognize and accept as legitimate, and in turn copresent interactants *determine* the sex and gender identities of others by reflexively placing them in an identity category that seems most intelligible and perceptible to them (Garrison 2018; Westbrook and Schilt 2014). In their daily activities, most people are recognized and thus determined to be either "female" or "male" through their construction of sex, gender, and sexual identities, and being held accountable to sex and gender identities is therefore unavoidable. Within socially structured interaction, then, we encourage and expect others to attribute to us a particular sex identity—to avoid negative assessments—and facilitate the ongoing task of accountability through demonstrating our sex and gender by means of concocted practices that may be interpreted accordingly. The specific meanings of sex, gender, and sexuality are defined in social interaction and therefore through personal practice. Routinely doing sex, gender, and sexuality renders social action accountable in terms of structurally available gender and sexual practices appropriate to one's sex identity in the specific social situations in which one acts. It is the particular structured sex, gender, and sexual relations in distinct settings that give behavior its sexed, gendered, and sexual meanings. What we term an "accountable identity," then, is a sex, gender, or sexual identity routinely legible and meaningful to oneself and/or others within and/or across particular contexts.

In this view, then, although people often reflexively decide quite early in life that they *are* a boy or a girl, and later adopt a routine identity as masculine or feminine and straight, gay, lesbian, bisexual, and so on, the actual everyday "doing" of sex, gender, and sexuality identities are accomplished systematically and are never a static or finished product. Rather, people fashion sex, gender, and sexual identities in specific social situations—they are best understood as fluid, contingent, provisional, and temporary constructions. People participate in reflexive self-regulating conduct whereby they monitor their own and others' embodied social actions and respond to and draw from available social structures. This perspective allows for innovation and flexibility in sex, gender, and sexual identities—and the ongoing potentiality of normative transgression—but simultaneously underscores the ever-present possibility of any sexed, gendered, and sexual identity being assessed (held accountable) by other social actors. Sex identity serves as a resource for the interpretation of situated social conduct, as copresent interactants in each setting attempt to hold accountable behavior as "female" or "male"—that is, socially defined membership in one sex category is used as a means of discrediting or accepting gender and sexual practices. And when individuals are unable to determine another person's sex, the particular identity is deemed unrecognizable—and thus unaccountable—to them, which thereby causes the person to lose their interactional personhood (Garrison 2018).

We situationally embody sex, gender, and sexuality according to our own unique experiences, and accountability is regulatory in the sense of attempting to maintain *congruence* among sex, gender, and sexual binaries. As Hollander writes specifically regarding gender: "The motivation for doing gender in everyday life . . . is people's knowledge that others may, at any moment, evaluate their behavior relative to normative conceptions of gender, whatever those mean in the given situation" (2018, 176). This implies that a *congruence* between perceived sex and gender identities is a crucial part of the social process of validating masculinity and femininity and, thus, accountable identities.

During social interaction, most people see sex and gender as a mutually constituted, inseparable, seamless whole; however, when we are unable to construct sex and gender in ways that copresent interactants recognize, they may challenge our performance, and/or we may question the authenticity of our own identities (Garrison 2018). Such *incongruency* between sex and gender can produce cognitive dissonance in copresent interactants, particularly for those minoritized by sex/gender accountability—such as masculine women, feminine men, and some identifying as transgender, nonbinary, or gender expansive—who also risk being punished (Pascoe 2007, 2013; Messerschmidt 2018a). Awareness of others' disapproval can prompt efforts to concoct sex and gender performances to avoid *binary misgendering* (in the case of binary transmen/women) or *nonbinary misgendering* (in the case of those who identify outside or beyond the gender binary) (cf. Lucal 1999; Schilt and Westbrook 2009; Pfeffer 2014; Darwin 2017; shuster 2017; Garrison 2018; Risman 2018b; Barbee and Schrock 2019). Pfeffer (2014) theorized the "misrecognition" prevalent among her sample of queer social actors, while shuster (2017, 483) theorized "discursive aggression" to describe how verbal interaction holds transgender and nonbinary people accountable to binary categories (which they label "other-enforcement accountability") and how transgender and nonbinary individuals hold themselves accountable through reflexively anticipating developing interactions (which they designate as "self-enforcement accountability"). Such behavior reflects and reinforces the hegemonic binary structures of sex/gender power and inequality. For some, however, sex and gender are incongruent and (can) lead to reflexive introspection.

It is also the case that in some social contexts *incongruence* between sex and gender is acceptable, even celebrated, and is therefore accountable within that particular social situation or context (e.g., Pfeffer 2012, 2014; Risman 2018b). And yet, when transgender and nonbinary people interact outside such trans-affirming social situations, the likelihood of misgendering, misrecognition, and discursive aggression increases (shuster 2017; Garrison 2018).

Nevertheless, the dominant sex/gender process of accountability begins prior to sexed and gendered social action through the involvement of the "*design* of the behavior itself. Only when people's behavior deviates significantly from what is expected, are they actually called to account for it; most of the time they *discipline* themselves through the anticipation of potential consequences" (Hollander 2018, 177, emphasis added).

The Symbiotic Relationship between Reflexivity and Routine

The dialectical relationship between "design" and "discipline," as Hollander (2018) writes, is how reflexivity and routine as coconstitutive social processes come into play. Sex, gender, and sexual identity construction results from individuals often—but not always—considering the content of their social practices and acting after internal deliberation about the purpose and consequence of their behavior (Messerschmidt 2018a). Although the concept of *reflexivity* has a long history within sociology and has been defined in multiple ways (e.g., Caron 2013), we follow Archer (2000, 2007) who refers to reflexivity as an emergent property that provides individuals with the capacity to engage in internal conversations about particular social experiences and to decide how to respond appropriately—individuals construct a dialogic interaction with themselves. As Archer argues, reflexivity involves internally mulling over specific social events and interactions, considering the emotional valence of such circumstances, prioritizing what matters most, and ultimately planning, deciding, and *designing* a response (Archer 2007). Archer argues that reflexivity is not simply "a window on the world, rather it is what determines our being in the world, though not in times and circumstances of our choosing" (2000, 318). Internal deliberations that result in agentic reflexive choices to act in particular ways are based on, and embedded in, the situationally structured available sex, gender, and sexual identities, relations, and discourses. Indeed, practice is the essence of both *relational* and *discursive* structures, and interactional accountability encourages internal deliberation about and subsequent accomplishment of sex, gender, and sexual appropriate practices—and thus accountable identities—in particular contexts.

Sex, gender, and sexual identities are reflexively accomplished with copresent interactants, yet to "do" sex, gender, and sexuality reflexively requires "carefully consider[ing] the content of one's actions and act[ing] only after careful consideration of the intent, content, and effects of one's behavior" (P. Y. Martin 2003, 356; see also P. Y. Martin 2006). Although social actors make reflexive choices to act in particular ways, reflexivity is based on the situationally embodied sex, gender, and sexual identities embedded within contextual relational and discursive social structures. Accountability encourages people to internally deliberate about and then "do" sex, gender, and sexuality appropriate to particular situations and contexts. And accountability and thus reflexivity come into a focus when agents are confronted with a unique social situation—such as a challenge to their sex, gender, or sexual identity.

Despite engaging in reflexivity by reflecting on discourses, relations, inter-actions, and identities *prior* to participating in social action, when certain sex, gender, and sexuality practices occur with sufficient accountable consistency, they become "disciplined" embodiments that are practiced routinely and that actively assist in the construction of accountable identities (i.e., Hollander 2018). Sex, gender, and sexual *routine*, and thus one's sex, gender, and sexual accountable identities, are necessarily influenced by prior practice. And when such practices are contextually accountable, they are likely to be repeated unreflexively. To understand sex, gender, and sexuality as identities suggests that much sex, gender, and sexual routines are agentic, yet often unreflexively constructed; they are conscious—yet unreflexive—self-activating practices that are continuous through time and space. The "doings" of sex, gender, and sexual identities are not expressed out of some internal essence but are inter-actionally and institutionally accomplished in ways that give the appearance of reflecting one's "true" essence (Connell 1987; Butler 1990; Lorber 1994).[7] Individuals maintain an unreflexive perception of each particular context and what each necessitates to embody properly and thereby accountably a routine identity—one's practices are subsumed within the body as discipline.

To act unreflexively—or without internal deliberation about and atten-tion to a specific practice—and thus routinely is to accept a particular social action without question or objection. And although routine practices are a common part of everyday life, reflexive deliberation creates conditions for social practice that can disrupt or maintain (and sometimes maintain while appearing to disrupt; e.g., Bridges 2014) routine sex, gender, and sexual identities and inequalities. Routine sex, gender, and sexual practices lead to accountable identity formations sustained in part through old and new forms of accountability, depending upon the social interactions among individuals and in particular contexts. And it is such accountable identity formations that are actively constituted *within* relational and discursive social structures, and such structures simultaneously are actively constituted *within* routine practice. As such, both reflexive and routine behavior formulate sex, gender, and sexual identities. Our aim in this book is to demonstrate how reflexive and unreflexive routine practices are symbiotically interconnected and mutually constitute various sex, gender, and sexual identities.

Because of accountability, many actors maintain particular forms of structured knowledge that shape routine and everyday sex, gender, and sexual identities without internal deliberation. Most people get up in the morning without reflecting on whether they are a "male" or "female," "man" or "woman." Self-attribution as members of a specific sex category becomes a primary mode by which individuals "choose" to relate to the world and construct themselves within it. Most eventually embody a particular sex category (over time and space) as an unreflexive routine social practice—many do not normally devote reflexive attention to their sex category. For example, people routinely follow a complex set of daily practices that unreflexively certify membership in a particular sex category—not only such things as shaving, makeup, and accessory conventions and clothing styles but also demeanor, bearing, and carriage. We do not dedicate attention to these particular social actions, and thus such routine practice is unreflexive. But these disciplined embodied routines easily go unrecognized as sex and gender practice. As they become recurring embodiments, they do so in mundane and routine ways, and one can fail to appreciate the labor they entail (e.g., Garfinkel 1967). Sex and gender accountability are generally sustained through such unreflexive sex, gender, and sexual routines.

Social actors routinely link sex, gender, and sexual practice with particular *social signs* associated with specific situations that become contextual prompts, fostering unreflexive routines. Repeated exposure to such signs helps reproduce sexed, gendered, and sexualized practices as routinized, accountable identities. Social signs are variously verbal, symbolic, embodied, material, and virtual. As one example, the presence or absence of particular elements of embodiment—such as beards and breasts—are social signs that guide—or actually may challenge—routine sex, gender, and sexual identities (i.e., Dozier 2005). Although the result is a fleeting and momentary reaction to such "reminders" (often unaccompanied by reflexivity), they assist in maintaining a routine accountable identity. Yet routine social action is always agentic because it is consciously and reflexively accessible to the individual and, thus, changeable. For example, if a particular unreflexive practice seems unjustified, unwarranted, or unaccountable, individuals might reflexively deliberate about the situation and change one's routine accordingly. Reflexive and unreflexive routine practices may also occur simultaneously during the same social process, enabling an understanding of routine "as achievement" (Schegloff 1986). And in this book, we additionally demonstrate how reflexive and routine practices transpire jointly, how they are separate but simultaneously intertwined, how routine concurrently enables attention to reflexivity by providing the cognitive space to do so, how reflexivity may initiate routine, and how routine may lead to reflexivity.

Reflexive and Routine Embodiment

As we have emphasized, constructing sex, gender, and sexual identities entails *embodied* reflexive and routine practices. We experience the social world *through* our bodies, and the very possibility of a social world rests upon our embodiment (Crossley 2001). As Iris Marion Young points out:

> It is the body in its orientation toward and action upon and within its surroundings that constitutes the initial meaning-given act. The body is the first locus of intentionality, as pure presence to the world and openness upon its possibilities. The most primordial intentional act is the motion of the body orienting itself with respect to and moving within its surroundings. (1990, 147–48)

We understand the world from our embodied place in it and our perceptual awareness of situational intercorporeal surrounding space. The body is a sensuous being—it perceives, it touches, and it feels; it is a lived body, and given that reflexivity consists of perceptual sensations, and routine involves consistent bodily practice, they are both part of the body and therefore not separate, disconnected actions. The mind and the body are inseparably linked—a binary divide is a fiction—and live together as one in the social construction of sex, gender, and sexual identities (Budgeon 2003). In this conceptualization, then, the body forms the whole of our being, and therefore, one's reflexive and routine practices are located within the body, which in turn acts, and is acted upon, within intercorporeal social environments. And in contemporary Global North societies, the body is central to the social construction of identities (Giddens 1991)—bodies impact the accountability of identities. A proficient body is necessary for social action, and therefore, embodied discipline is fundamental to the competent and accountable social agent: "It is integral to the very nature both of agency and of being accepted (trusted) by others as competent" (Giddens 1991, 100).

Through reflexive and routine embodied social action, individuals construct sex, gender, and sexual identities (while simultaneously reproducing social structures) and present such identities as discursive and material resources for others as a consequence of their embodiment. Bodies and identities are thus irreducibly linked because bodies impact the negotiation and practice of identities, and thus, different bodies correspond to different identities (Budgeon 2003). The social situations in which embodied actions are oriented "are populated by others and it is these others, in part, towards whom the actions are oriented. Action is other oriented" (Crossley 1995, 141). In this way, social contexts are best understood as *intercorporeal*, involving interactions among situationally embodied people. Embodied social action is embedded within the specific social structural context of the agent, so that what we actually conceptualize are social situations that require specific "practical accommodation from our action" (136)—we reflexively and routinely respect, acknowledge, reproduce, and sometimes resist structured embodied practices. And as Goffman (1979, 6) acutely observes, such embodied identities are situational forms of "social portraiture" by which individuals discursively convey information that "the others in the gathering will need in order to manage their own courses of action—which knowledgeability [they] in turn must count on in carrying out [their] own designs." Doing sex, gender, and sexuality accountably is thus necessarily reflexive, routine, and intercorporeal; they are recognizable, intelligible, acceptable, and embodied.

Bodies are active in the production and transmission of social structures as well as embodied social actions and based on the reaction of others to our embodiments—whether or not embodiment is judged accountable is important to our sense of practicing accountable identities. Embodied accountability is vital to an individual's situational recognition as a competent social agent. If one's embodied appearance and practice are categorized by others as "failed," that degradation may result in a spoiled and unaccountable identity (Goffman 1968). Consequently, adequate participation in social life depends upon the successful reflexive and routine presenting, monitoring, interpreting, and reading of bodies as well as situationally and contextually appropriate embodied responses to such reading.

Goffman helps us understand how constructing sex, gender, and sexual identities is socially structured in the sense that we accomplish each bodily and in a manner that is accountable to situationally populated others. Individuals exhibit embodied sex, gender, and sexual competence through their appearance and by producing situationally appropriate routine "behavioral styles" that respond properly to the styles produced by others. In other words, "competent" individuals develop an embodied capacity to provide and to read structured depictions of sex, gender, and sexual identities in particular settings, and appropriate body management is crucial to smooth the flow of interaction essential to satisfactory attribution and accountability by others. To be "read" by others as male, female, masculine, feminine, straight, gay, lesbian, and so on, individuals must ensure that their proffered identities are maintained through situationally appropriate embodied display and behavior.

Additionally, however, properly accountable bodies construct relational and discursive social structures, and they signal and facilitate through their appearance and action the reflexive and routine maintenance of sex, gender, and sexual hegemonic binary power dynamics. Suitably adorned and comported bodies constitute the "shadow and the substance" of unequal sex, gender, and sexual relations (Goffman 1979, 6):

> The expression of subordination and domination through the swarm of situational means is more than a mere tracing of symbol or ritualistic affirmation of social hierarchy. These expressions considerably constitute the hierarchy; they are the shadow and the substance. (Goffman 1979, 6)

Individuals produce (and at times challenge) hegemonic binary relations through their embodied appearance and action.

The body is an essential part of sex, gender, and sexual practices in which we fashion appearance and actions to create properly and situationally adorned and performed embodied identities. The body is an inescapable and integral part of doing sex, gender, and sexual identities, entailing social practice that constantly refers to bodies and what bodies do; it is not social practice reduced to the body (Connell 2000). Constructing hegemonic relations involves a dialectical relationship by which practice deals with the biological characteristics of bodies: "It gives them a social determination. The connection between social and natural structures is one of practical relevance, not causation" (Connell 1987, 78).

In the social construction of, for example, hegemonic masculinities and emphasized femininities, bodily similarities between men and women are negated and suppressed, whereas bodily differences are exaggerated (Connell and Messerschmidt 2005). The body is essential to, for example, the binary discursive structure of "two and only two sexes." The body is significant for our sense of accountable identities that we reflexively and routinely sustain through time and space. Bodies and thus identities are continually in the process of becoming, made and remade simultaneously (Budgeon 2003). Bodies impact our recurring self-attributions and thus one's accountable identity as male or female, masculine or feminine, straight or gay, and so on. Because "sex" is culturally associated with genitalia, there is likely to be a degree of social standardization of individual lives—we recursively construct ourselves as, for example, an embodied "boy/man" or as an embodied "girl/woman," and such sexed identities constrain and enable social action. For most people, sex is the primary claimed identity that is relatively solid and unchanging while gender and sexuality qualify sex (Paechter 2006). Nevertheless, some challenge this process—such as certain nonbinary people—whereby sex is the qualifier and gender the primary mode through which one relates to the world (Paechter 2006, 259).

Bodies participate in social action by unreflexively delineating courses of social conduct: Bodies are agents of social practice and, given the context, will do certain things and not others; our bodies are constraints and enablers of social action, and therefore they situationally mediate and influence the social construction of identities (Connell 1995).[8] The body often is lived in terms of what it can "do" and the "consequence of [routine] bodily practice is historicity: the creation and transformation of situations. Bodies are drawn into history and history is constituted through bodies" (Connell 1998, 7). In short, the body actively participates in the shaping and generating of sex, gender, and sexual identities and thus unequal relations.

Structured Action

Although we have emphasized social interaction, accountability, social signs, and embodiment, we also acknowledge the structural sex, gender, and sexual relations and discourses that affect both routine and reflexive practice. Social structures are reproduced through everyday sex, gender, and sexual practices (Connell 1987; Lorber 1994; P. Y. Martin 2003, 2004; Risman 2004, 2018a, 2018b). In other words, agents draw upon social structures to engage in social action and in turn reproduce (and sometimes challenge) social structures through embodied and accountable sexed, gendered, and sexual identities (e.g., Connell 1987; Lorber 1994; P. Y. Martin 2001, 2004, 2006; Messerschmidt 2018a; Risman 2004, 2018a, 2018b).

Social structures are recurring routine patterned practices and discourses that tend to transcend time and space and that constrain and enable behavior in contextually specific ways, yet "only exist as the reproduced conduct of situated actors" (Giddens 1976, 127). And as stated earlier in "Theory and Method," it is accountable social practices and identity formations that constitute social structures, and such structures simultaneously are embodied actively within routine practices and identities. Social structures require continued acceptance and embodied production to persist. In such duality, structure and action are inseparable as "knowledgeable" human agents of sex, gender, and sexual identities enact social structures by reflexively and routinely putting into practice their structured knowledge. Social structures are thus both the "medium" and "outcome" of social action: *medium* because they are the embodiment of social structures within social action and *outcome* because it is through social action that social structures are reproduced—and sometimes transformed—in time and space (Giddens 1976; Connell 1987).

Because agents reflexively and routinely "do" sex, gender, and sexual identities in specific socially structured situations, they reproduce and sometimes change social structures. And given that agents often reproduce sex, gender, and sexual identities in socially structured specific practices, there are a variety of ways to accomplish them. Within specific social structural settings, particular forms of sex, gender, and sexual identities are embodied and thereby available and accountable. Accordingly, sexed, gendered, and sexual *agency* must be viewed as reflexively and routinely embodied structured action—what people, and therefore bodies, do under specific social structural conditions that are variously constraining and enabling (Messerschmidt 2018a).

Although there exists a variety of social structures, two are especially useful for conceptualizing sex, gender, and sexual identity formations: relational and discursive (Messerschmidt 2018a). *Relational* social structures establish through social practice the interconnections and interdependence among/ between individuals in particular contexts and define social relationships among people in terms of sex, gender, and sexuality. Relational social structures constrain and enable social action. Examples of relational social structures are the informal yet unequal network of sexed, gendered, and sexual "cliques" in elementary and secondary schools; the sex, gender, and sexual divisions of labor in workplaces; and the hegemonic binaries of sex, gender, and sexuality. Conversely, *discursive* social structures refer to representations, ideas, and sign systems (language) that produce culturally significant meaning. Discursive social structures establish through social practice orders of "truth" and what is accepted as "reality" in particular situations. Like relational social structures, discursive social structures constrain and enable the possibilities of social action. Examples of discursive social structures are the notion of two and only two sexes, genders, and sexualities; beliefs of masculine primacy; social conventions defining styles of dress, interests, behavior; and adornments in terms of sex, gender, and sexuality.

Both relational and discursive social structures are constituted through social action and concurrently constitute practice by fostering contextually shared meanings, frequently operating in combination, though sometimes toward contradictory ends.[9] Structured action simultaneously produces particular social relations *and* social meanings that are culturally salient because they shape a sense of what is (un)acceptable—that is, what is (un) accountable in specific contexts. Through embodied social action, individuals produce relational social structures that concurrently proffer meaningful representations (through embodied appearance and practices) for others as a consequence of their social action. And in turn, through embodied social action individuals also produce discursive social structures that concurrently constitute social relations (through representations, ideas, and sign systems) for others as a consequence of their social action. In other words, discursive social structures often are a part of relational social structures, and the latter often are a component of the former.

The mutual constitution of relational and discursive social structures in part establishes the sex, gender, and sexual knowledge we rely on to engage in particular forms of social action—to reflexively and routinely mobilize specific configurations of sex, gender, and sexual identities. For example, structured relational hegemonic binaries coexist with structured discourses of two and only two sexes, genders, and sexualities. To be sure, copresent inter-actants "see" both relational and discursive structures embodied in identity formations, and it is that perception that results in (un)accountability.

Nevertheless, relational and discursive social structures are not all encom-passing, and neither are they always accepted without question, objection, or challenge (e.g., Lucal 1999; Pfeffer 2012; Darwin 2017; shuster 2017; Barbee and Schrock 2019). As Connell (1987, 95) puts it, "practice can be turned against what constrains it; so, structure can be deliberately the object of practice." Through reflexivity, then, some attempt to distance themselves from particular aspects of social structures, which clears the path for innova-tion and change. When confronting social structures, agents at times engage in reflexive internal deliberations and may decide to break from structures. And when such a disconnect between agent from structure transpires, the result often is unique forms of social action. As we discuss later in "Theory and Method," nonhegemonic sex, gender, and sexual identities are rapidly changing, especially for youth, which reject and thus challenge existing hegemonic binaries.

Sex, Gender, and Sexual Hegemony

Power is an important structural feature of sex, gender, and sexual identities. Socially structured power relations among and between gendered actors are constructed historically on the bases of sex, gender, and sexual preference (Connell 1987). In other words, in specific contexts some men and some women have greater power than other men or other women; some genders have greater power than other genders; some sexualities have greater power than other sexualities; and the capacity to exercise power and "do" sex, gen-der, and sexual identities is, for the most part, a reflection of one's place in sex, gender, and sexual structured relations of power. Consequently, in general, for example, men, masculinity, and heterosexuality exercise greater power than other sex categories, genders, and sexualities. Power, then, is a relationship that structures social interaction not only between men and women but also among men and among women as well as in terms of gender and sexuality (Connell 1987, 1995). Nevertheless, power is not absolute and at times may actually shift in relation to different axes of power and powerlessness.[10]

Both sex and gender hegemony of course constitute a power relation and involve those sexes and genders that *legitimate* an unequal *relationship* between men and women, masculinity and femininity, and among masculinities. The emphasis on *legitimation* underscores the achievement of sex and gender hegemony through cultural influence and discursive persuasion, encouraging consent and compliance—rather than direct control and commands—to unequal sex and gender relations. From this, sex and gender hegemonic configurations of practice construct both relational and discursive social structures because they establish relations of sex and gender inequality and at once signify discursively acceptable (and accountable) understandings of sex and gender relations.

In this regard, Mimi Schippers's (2007) work is significant because it opens an extremely useful approach of conceptualizing how such *legitimacy* in sex and gender hegemony transpires. Schippers (2007, 90) argues that embedded within the meanings of structured sex and gendered relationships are the qualities that members of each sex category should and are assumed to possess. Therefore, it is in "the idealized *quality content* of the categories 'man' and 'woman' that we find the hegemonic significance of masculinity and femininity." For Schippers, certain masculine characteristics work to *legitimate* men's power over women "when they are symbolically paired with a complementary and inferior quality attached to femininity" (91).[11] The significance of hegemonic forms of masculinity then is found in discursive meanings that legitimate a rationale for structured social relations and that ensure the ascendancy and power of men as well as specific configurations of masculinities. What Schippers highlights, therefore, is first the *relationship* between masculinity and femininity and, second, how certain masculinities are hegemonic only when they articulate discursively particular *gender qualities* that are *complementary* and *hierarchical* in relation to specific feminine qualities. For example, such a complementary and hierarchical relationship might establish masculinity as constituting physical strength, the ability to use interpersonal violence in the face of conflict, and authority, whereas femininity would embrace physical vulnerability, an inability to use violence effectively, and compliance (91). When both masculine and feminine qualities legitimate a complementary and hierarchical relationship between them, we have *gender hegemony*, involving unequal gender (and usually sexed) relations or the superordinate position of men and masculinity and subordinate position of women and femininity (94).

This concentration on *gendered quality content* empirically enables investigating multiple forms of sex and gender hegemony because *whenever a complementary and hierarchical relationship between masculinity and femininity exists, gender (and often sexed) hegemony prevails.*[12] To be sure, "gendered quality content" does *not* mean "fixed character traits"; rather, it refers to changing *relational* attributes in sundry historical and social situations.

Where we part from Schippers is in her argument that there exists "neither pariah masculinities nor subordinate masculinities," because "masculinity must always remain superior; it must never be conflated with something undesirable" (Schippers 2007, 96). Schippers makes this point when discussing, *exclusively*, men who embody culturally defined *feminine* qualities (i.e., having erotic desire for men; seemingly weak, ineffectual, and compliant), yet ignoring those men who embody noxious and harmful masculine qualities. In other words, Schippers's perspective fails to account for masculine *relationships* based similarly on differing gendered qualities attached to each and that *legitimate* a hierarchical relationship between two or more different types of masculinities. Although the application of *quality content* to discern gender hegemony discursively is significant, we extend Schippers's conception of gender hegemony to include *gendered qualities* that establish and legitimate a hierarchical (but not necessarily complementary) relationship to nonhegemonic masculinities (see Bridges 2014).

Sex and gender hegemonies form relational and discursive social structures that have cultural influence but do not entirely determine social action. Sex and gender hegemonies often, but not always, underpin the conventions applied in the enactment and reproduction of masculinities and femininities—the lived embodied patterns of meanings, which as they are experienced as practice, appear as reciprocally confirming. Sex and gender hegemonies relationally and discursively shape a sense of "reality" for sexed and gendered actors in specific situations and are continually renewed, re-created, defended, and modified through social action. And yet, so too is it possible at times to resist, limit, alter, and challenge them.

The diversity and wide variety of, for example, hegemonic masculinities and emphasized femininities operate as components of sex and gender relational and discursive structures, constituting recurring "on-hand" meaningful practices and discourses that are culturally influential and thus available to be actualized into social action in a range of different circumstances (Messerschmidt 2018a). Messerschmidt defines *hegemonic masculinities* as those masculinities embodied locally, regionally, and globally that legitimate an unequal relationship between men and women, masculinity and femininity, and among masculinities (see also Connell and Messerschmidt 2005). Hegemonic masculinity has no meaning outside its relationship to emphasized femininity—and nonhegemonic masculinities—or that form of femininity that is practiced in a complementary, compliant, and accommodating subordinate relationship with hegemonic masculinity. The emphasis here is on hegemonic masculinity as always already constituting an unequal practice-based relationship with emphasized femininity that legitimates sex and gender inequality. In other words, both the relational and legitimation features are central, involving a certain form of embodied masculinity in unequal relation to a certain type of embodied femininity (as well as embodied nonhegemonic masculinities). And it is the unequal relationship between superordination and subordination whereby sex and gender hegemony are legitimated. That is, hegemonic masculinities acquire their legitimacy by embodying culturally supported "superior" sex/gender practices in relation to the embodiment of culturally supported "inferior" sex/gender practices. In other words, certain culturally defined and *practiced* "superior" masculine qualities legitimate unequal sex and gender relations when they are symbolically paired with culturally defined "inferior" *practices* attached to femininity.

As such, hegemonic masculinities and emphasized femininities are essentially *decentered*. There exists neither one nor a few hegemonic masculinities and emphasized femininities; rather, they are multifarious and found in a whole variety of settings—locally, regionally, and globally. Hegemonic masculinities and emphasized femininities do not discriminate in terms of race/ethnicity, class, age, sexuality, and nationality, and do not represent a certain *type* of man or woman but, rather, personify and symbolize an unequal *relationship* between men and women, between masculinity and femininity, and among masculinities that is widely dispersed and operates both intimately and diffusely.

Such copious sex and gender hegemonies provide a conceptual framework that is materialized in the design of daily embodied practices, interactions, and discourses. As individuals construct hegemonic masculinities and emphasized femininities, for example, they simultaneously present those unequal relations as culturally significant for others as a consequence of their embodied reflexive and routine social action. Sex and gendered power, then, are both "top down" and "disciplinary" (Foucault 1979) and are constituted through acceptance of, and consent to, sex and gendered hegemonic forms of meanings, knowledge, and practice that are ubiquitous locally, regionally, and globally.

Additionally, the relationship between sex and gender hegemony underpins sexual hegemony, or what has become known as *heteronormativity*—the legal, cultural, organizational, and interpersonal practices that derive from and reinforce the relational and discursive structures that there are two and only two naturally opposite and complementary sexes, that gender is a natural manifestation of sex, and that it is natural for the two opposite and complementary sexes to be sexually attracted to each other. In other words, the social construction of sex differences is mutually constituted with the assumption of gender and sexual complementarity, or the notion that men's and women's bodies are naturally compatible and thus "made for each other" (Jackson and Scott 2010). Heterosexuality is understood culturally as the "natural" erotic attraction to sex/gender difference, as well as a natural practice of male active dominance and female passive receptivity, and thus this notion of "natural attraction and practice" reinforces sex and gender hegemony as innate, complementary, and hierarchical (Schippers 2007). Heteronormativity therefore refers to "the myriad ways in which heterosexuality is produced as a natural, unproblematic, taken-for-granted, ordinary phenomenon" (Kitzinger 2005, 478) and captures at once hegemonic sex, gender, and sexual binaries.

Accordingly, there is nothing "natural" about heterosexuality, and indeed the term "heterosexuality" actually did not appear until the 1890s, and then it was used to specifically designate an identity based not on procreation but rather on lascivious sexual desire (Katz 1990).[13] Heterosexuality became disconnected from procreation, and "normal" sexuality was henceforth defined as opposite-sex attraction; "abnormal" sexuality was same-sex attraction. The concept of heterosexuality was defined in terms of its relationship to the concept (and diagnosis) of homosexuality, both terms categorizing a sexual desire unrelated to procreation, and individuals now began to define their sexual identity according to whether they were attracted to the same or the opposite sex (e.g., D'Emilio 1993). And Steven Seidman articulates well the historically constructed close connection between gender and heterosexuality:

> There can be no norm of heterosexuality, indeed no notion of heterosexuality, without assuming two genders that are coherent as a relationship of opposition and unity. If there were no fixed categories of gender, if there were no "men" and "women," there could be no concept of heterosexuality! So, heterosexuality is anchored by maintaining a gender order through either celebrating and idealizing gender or by stigmatizing and polluting gender nonconformity. (Seidman 2010, 158)

Sex, gender, and sexual hegemony are mutually constituted so that men, masculinity, and heterosexuality are deemed "superior" and women, femininity, and homosexuality (and nonhegemonic sexes, genders, and sexualities, see below) are judged to be "inferior." The heteronormative social construction of men and women as naturally different, complementary, and hierarchical sanctions heterosexuality as *the* normal and natural form of sexuality and masculine men and feminine women as *the* normal and natural sex and gender presentation. Heteronormativity then reproduces a sexual social structure based on an unequal sexual binary—heterosexuality and homosexuality—and that is dependent upon the alleged natural sexual attraction of two and only two opposite and complementary sexes that in turn constructs heteromasculine men and heterofeminine women difference. Nevertheless, some heterosexual practices are more powerful than others. As Connell writes, "Hegemonic heterosexuality, then, is not a natural fact but a state of play in a field of power and cathexis" (1987, 161). That is, normative heterosexuality determines its own social structure and thus internal boundaries as well as marginalizing and sanctioning sexualities outside those boundaries.[14]

In addition to sexuality, structured action theory emphasizes the construction of race, class, age, and nationality as situated social, interactional, variable, and embodied identity accomplishments mutually constituted with sex, gender, and sexual identities. Building on previous scholarship (e.g., Connell 1987; Hames-Garcia 2011; Ken 2010; Ken and Helmuth 2021; Tapley 2013), we maintain that *mutual constitution* takes place when two or more sex, gender, race, class, age, sexuality, and nationality identities are accomplished together through the same practice, and their joint configuration materializes a particular embodied identity.

In this book we exclusively concentrate on sex, gender, and sexuality, and when any mixture of these three identities is accomplished together through the same practice, their collaborative composition forms a specific embodied identity. For example, within particular contexts—such as elementary and junior high school—the accomplishment together of sex category (girl) and gender (masculinity) identities in the same practice mutually constitutes an embodied "tomboy" identity. In other words, the mutual constitution of sex and gender identities in the same practices enables—or makes possible—the actuation of a particularized identity. We know that this mutual constitution takes place because copresent interactants successfully and simultaneously "read" the two identity formations as intended through practice and place the actor within a specific identity category—a "tomboy." Individuals embody their various identities in concert, they are accomplished together as indivisible features of a seamless whole, and the particular identity is recognized as accountable (or unaccountable) by others. And it is such embodiment that helps construct—relationally and discursively—socially structured sex, gender, and sexual relational and discursive inequalities.

Sex, gender, and sexual identities grow out of embodied social practices in specific unequal structural settings and serve to inform other identity practices episodically in reciprocal relation. The result is the ongoing social construction of sex, gender, and sexual identities as variably constituted by each other. In other words, the significance of each accomplishment to particular forms of sex, gender, and sexual identities is socially situated and thus intermittent. Indeed, sex, gender, and sexual hegemony only exist as the replicated practices of situated embodied identities—it is through the mutual constitution of identities that social structures are (re)produced. Yet it is also through such a mutual constitution of identities that social structures are challenged, resisted, and reformed.[15]

Nonhegemonic Sexes, Genders, and Sexualities

In addition to variable mutual constitution of sex, gender, and sexual identities with each other, structured action theory recognizes distinct nonhegemonic sexes, genders, and sexualities. First, there exist dominant, dominating, subordinate, and positive genders (Messerschmidt 2018a). Messerschmidt refers to *dominant* masculinities and femininities as distinct from hegemonic masculinities and emphasized femininities in that they are not always associated with and linked to gender hegemony but refer fundamentally to the most celebrated, common, or current form of masculinity and femininity in a particular social setting. Conversely, *dominating* masculinities and femininities are similar to dominant masculinities and femininities but differ in the sense that they involve commanding and controlling specific interactions and exercising power and control over people and events. Dominant and dominating masculinities and femininities do not necessarily legitimate a hierarchical relationship between men and women, masculinity and femininity. Although hegemonic masculinities and emphasized femininities at times may also be *dominant* or *dominating*, dominant and dominating masculinities and femininities are never hegemonic or emphasized if they fail culturally to *legitimate* unequal gender relations. In this latter scenario, dominant and dominating masculinities/femininities are thereby constructed *outside* relations of gender hegemony; however, dominant and dominating masculinities and femininities necessarily acquire meaning only in relation to other masculinities and femininities (Messerschmidt 2018a).

Dominant and dominating masculinities and femininities exhibit different logics and degrees of power. For masculinities in particular, dominant masculinities may construct, for instance, celebratory power, while dominating masculinities fashion commanding and controlling power; neither in and of themselves orchestrate hegemonic masculine power. Although it is true that hegemonic masculinities may not always be dominant and dominating in the above sense, the reverse also holds: in addition to their legitimating influence, hegemonic masculinities may concurrently be socially dominant and/or dominating. It is crucial, therefore, to leave open investigative room for empirical exploration as to when, how, and under what particular social conditions hegemonic masculinities are simultaneously dominant and/or dominating, and when they are not.

Subordinate masculinities and femininities refer to those masculinities and femininities situationally constructed as lesser than or aberrant and deviant to hegemonic masculinity or emphasized femininity as well as dominant/dominating masculinities and femininities (i.e., Connell 1987, 1995). Depending upon the particular context, such subordination can be conceptualized in terms of, for example, race, class, age, sexualities, or nationality. Although

homophobia has transformed radically in recent years in Global North societies, it clearly has not disappeared (e.g., Diefendorf and Bridges 2020).
Arguably, then, a form of subordination is that of gay boys/men and lesbian
girls/women—still today, frequently the former is culturally feminized and
the latter culturally masculinized. In a heteronormative hegemonic binary
culture, gay identity, performance, and culture continue to be socially defined
in many contexts as the embodiment of content qualities expelled from configurations of hegemonic masculinity and emphasized femininity.

Related to this, a second form of subordination usually occurs if there
exists *incongruence* within the sex-gender-sexuality interconnection. For
example, girls and women perceived as female who construct "incongruent"
bodily practices defined as masculine—such as expressing sexual desire
for girls, acting sexually promiscuous, and/or presenting as authoritarian,
physically aggressive, or taking charge—are viewed as polluting "normal"
and "natural" hegemonic gender and sexual relations and often are verbally,
socially, and physically subordinated (Schippers 2007). Similarly, individuals
perceived as male but who construct "incongruent" bodily practices defined
as feminine—such as sexually desiring boys or simply practicing celibacy;
being passive, compliant, or shy; and/or being physically weak or unadven-
turous—likewise are seen as polluting "normal" and "natural" hegemonic
gender and sexual relations and often are verbally, socially, and physically
subordinated. Simply put, social structures that actualize unequal gender and
sexual relations are sustained in part through the subordination of specific
"transgressive" configurations of gender and sexuality.

A third form of subordination often occurs among individuals who construct situationally accountable masculinities and femininities. For example,
the masculinity of a son may be judged to be subordinate to the *dominant*
masculinity of his father, and the femininity of a daughter may be considered
subordinate to the *dominant* femininity of her mother. Both of these are subordinate primarily by reason of age, not because of any incongruence between
sex and gender, and usually are established and thus practiced independent
of gender hegemony.

Finally, sex, gender, and sexual identities are rapidly changing, especially for youth, who increasingly reject the hegemonic binaries of male/
female, masculinity/femininity, and heterosexual/homosexual identified
earlier. There now exists a multiplicity of nonbinary sex, gender, and sexual
identities, providing a broader range of displays, practices, and desires. For
increasing numbers of people throughout the last decade—who feel unable
to identify with and "fit" easily into the hegemonic binaries—they express
differently the ways in which sex, gender, and sexuality are conceptualized,
enacted, embodied, represented, and practiced (Cover 2019). A few examples

of these new sex, gender, and sexual identities that extend beyond the hegemonic binaries include the following (Cover 2019):

Sex: *androgynous* (individuals who maintain both male and female bodily characteristics); *demiboy/girl* (individuals who feel only partly male or female, regardless of their assigned sex at birth); and *intersex* (people born with reproductive/sexual anatomy that do not neatly fit hegemonic sex categorizations)

Gender: *genderqueer* (individuals assigned female or male at birth but identify as both masculine and feminine or as neither masculine nor feminine); *maxigender* (people who embody all available genders simultaneously); and *transfeminine* (individuals assigned male at birth but identify as feminine)

Sexuality: *demisexual* (individuals who do not experience sexual attraction unless they form a strong emotional connection with someone); *pansexual* (individuals who are sexually attracted to people regardless of their sex or gender identities); and *skoliosexual* (people sexually attracted to individuals who practice nonbinary gender, regardless of their sex)

This list represents only a small sample of some of the newly proliferating sex, gender, and sexual identities in the Global North. These new identities symbolize a real need among an increasing number of people to practice more precisely and comprehensively sex, gender, and sexuality (Cover 2019). Such nonhegemonic nonbinary identities challenge hegemonic binary sex, gender, and sexual identities and, thus, are frequently subjected to subordination through discrimination, marginalization, harassment, stigmatization, ridicule, opprobrium, and violence (Lorber 2018; Worthen 2020, 2021; Nadal et al. 2016).

For old and new nonhegemonic subordinated identities, certain occasions present themselves as more effectively intimidating for demonstrating and affirming embodied sex, gender, and sexuality. In certain contexts, individuals may experience through the actions of others body betrayal and, subsequently, may be identified as embodying sex, gender, and sexual identity "failure." The constitution of sex, gender, and sexual identities through reflexive and routine bodily appearance and performance means that sex, gender, and sexual accountability are vulnerable when the situationally and socially structured appropriate appearance and performance are not (for whatever reason) sustained. Because the taken-for-granted sex, gender, and sexuality of individuals can be challenged in certain contexts, each may become particularly salient. They are, as Morgan (1992, 47) would put it, "more or less explicitly put on the line," and the responding social action can generate an intensified reflexivity and a distinct type of social action.

Challenges to and subordination of particular identities are contextually embodied interactions that result in, for example, sex, gender, or sexual degradation—the individual is constructed as a subordinated "deviant" member of society. Such identity challenges and subordination arise from interactional threats, insults, and violence from peers, teachers, parents, workmates, or strangers and from situationally and bodily defined expectations that are not achievable. *Identity challenges*, then, in various ways, proclaim certain individuals and identities subordinate (and thus unaccountable) in contextually defined embodied terms. Such challenges and subordinations may motivate social action toward specific situationally embodied practices that attempt to correct the subordinating social situation and become accountable (Messerschmidt 2018a).[16] Given that such interactions question, undermine, and/or threaten one's sex, gender, or sexual identity, for some only certain embodied practices can overcome the challenge, and the result is often a new identity formation. The existence of identity challenges alerts us to the transitory and fluid nature of sex, gender, and sexual identities, and to how particular forms of social action may arise as embodied practices when identities are contested.

Finally, *positive* masculinities and femininities are those that legitimate an egalitarian relationship between men and women, between masculinity and femininity, and among masculinities and femininities and, therefore, are constructed exterior to sex and gender hegemonic relational and discursive structures in any particular setting. Such masculinities and femininities do not assume a normal and natural relationship to sex and sexuality and usually are not constructed as naturally complementary.

Social action is never simply an autonomous event but is amalgamated into larger assemblages—what we will discuss as socially structured *reflexive* and *routine* embodied identities. These embodied identities encourage specific lines of social action, and relational and discursive social structures shape the capacities from which social actions are routinely constructed over time. People negotiate the situations that face them in everyday life and in the process pursue sex, gender, and sexual identities. From this perspective, then, social action is often—but not always—reflexively designed with an eye to one's sex, gender, and sexual accountability individually, bodily, situationally, and structurally. Structured action theory, then, permits us to explore how and in what respects reflexive and routine embodied identities and unequal sex, gender, and sexual relations and discourses are constituted in certain settings at certain times. To understand the multifarious sexes, genders, and sexualities, we are interested here in describing how, specifically, structure and action are woven inextricably into ongoing reflexive and routine practices.

Structured action theory sanctions the investigation of different ways individuals experience their everyday worlds from their particular positions in society and how they relate to various others. This theory identifies embodied hegemonic and nonhegemonic sexes, genders, and sexualities variably accomplished together and thus as mutually constituted by each other as well as by race, class, age, nationality, and more. Structured action theory also recognizes how sex, gender, and sexual identities are associated with the specific intercorporeal contexts of individual action, and they are for the most part self-regulated—through reflexive and routine practices—within that context. Social actors reflexively self-regulate their behavior and make specific choices in particular socially structured contexts. In this way, then, people construct varieties of sex, gender, and sexual specific embodied identities. And by emphasizing diversity in sex, gender, and sexual identities, we achieve a more fluid and situated approach to our understanding of embodied reflexive and routine practice.

METHOD

The two life stories discussed in "Identity Reminiscences" are part of a larger study that investigates people who self-identify as *genderqueer*, a relatively recent gender identity that challenges the sex, gender, and sexual hegemonic binaries. The participants comprise a variety of individuals who were assigned female at birth but who now identify as *both* masculine and feminine, as *neither* masculine nor feminine, or something else. Mutually constituting both genders or having no exclusively single gender at all, genderqueer individuals challenge the hegemonic binaries and live in sex, gender, and sexual expansive ways that challenge traditional sex, gender, and sexual assumptions. In "Identity Reminiscences," we outline the data generated through the two detailed life-history interviews.

Detailed Life Histories

In 2010 and 2011, the lead author completed in-depth interviews with fourteen white, working- and middle-class genderqueer people, all of whom were assigned female at birth, and who now associate with LGBTQ+ and/or transmasculine communities. The two groups of genderqueers ("both" and "neither") were studied in the context of their entire lives, from their earliest memories to the point at which the lead author encountered them. Such life-history accounts generate an understanding of the stages and crucial periods in the social processes of development, and to an understanding of how the particular individual is both enabled and constrained by social context.

Thus, this study contributes significantly to our understanding of the diversity of sex, gender, and sexual identities in society today.

While we analyze some of the similarities and differences among and between the genderqueer identifying individuals in this study, we are explicitly not making claims about what genderqueer identities are or attempting to generalize from these two life histories. Rather, through these life histories we seek to investigate the relationship between reflexibility and routine in shaping sex, gender, and sexual practices, a process on magnified display in this study. Nevertheless, to comprehend what it is about certain individuals who declare a genderqueer identity, we must comprehend the social construction of sex, gender, and sexuality—how a sex/gender/sexuality nexus may be a meaningful social construct and embodied practice in particular settings.

The primary goal of this study is to glean considerable and telling information from a modest sample of people from various adult age groups who declared a genderqueer identity. By analyzing each detailed life history, the study has at least two significant strengths. First, this study is distinct in its emphasis on people who begin in a similar way—assigned female at birth— yet come to identify in a different way: as either a "both" or a "neither" genderqueer. The two case studies discussed in "Identity Reminiscences" help distinguish between these different genderqueer projects. Second, the life-history method is particularly relevant because it richly documents personal experiences and transformations over time. A life history records the relation between the social conditions that determine practice and the future social world that practice brings into being. The life-history method is what Thomas and Znaniecki ([1927] 1958) characterized as the "perfect" type of social science material. Indeed, the life-history method has experienced a resurgence in the social sciences, due in part to the fact that life histories tap continuous "lived experiences" of individuals. That is, the method demands a close evaluation of the meaning of social life for those who enact it—revealing their experiences, embodied practices, and social world. As Orbuch (1997, 455) points out in her important article "People's Accounts Count," the life history is significant sociologically because we gain "insight into human experience and arrive at meanings or culturally embedded normative explanations," insight that allows us to understand "the ways in which people organize views of themselves, of others, and of their social world."

The social process of declaring a genderqueer identity can be understood through a reconstruction of the life history that relates later events to earlier interactions and practices (Connell 1987). Such life-history accounts are "destined to bring to light" the embodied practices by which individuals declare themselves genderqueer (Sartre 1956, 734). Notwithstanding that life-history research is difficult and time consuming, it is an extraordinarily fruitful method for sex, gender, and sexuality analysis.

In addition to in-depth documentation of an individual's social world and representations of interaction and embodied practice, the life history links the social and historical context in which both are embedded. In most sex, gender, and sexuality research, data is generated only cross-sectionally, at one point in time; however, life-history studies notably uncover patterns unfolding as trajectories through time, and therefore the researcher is able to "see" each life history genuinely as a changing pattern of reflexive and routine identities through time and space. The fluidity documented in a life history is itself the relation between the social conditions that determine practice and the future social world that practice brings into being. That is to say, the life-history method always concerns the making of social life through time. And one salient feature of the life-history method in exploring genderqueer people is that it permits an in-depth understanding of the interplay between relational and discursive structures and reflexive and routine personal practices.

The life history can reveal what other methods hide or obscure. And this study specifically investigates social cognition, or how individual interviewees process and apply social knowledge about social interactions, social structures, and social situations—this study is an example of cognitive sociology at work. The study focuses particularly on the changing symbiotic relationship between reflexive and routine sex, gender, and sexual identities and projects throughout one's life; how the body is a participant in the shaping and generating of sex, gender, and sexual identities; how any combinations of sex, gender, and sexual identities are accomplished together through the same practice and their mutual constitution forms a specific embodied identity; and how identities are actively constituted within relational and discursive structures and such structures are actively present within reflexive and routine practices.

Sample

Life-history research does not target large and representative samples from which to draw bold generalizations. Rather, in this study the goal is to uncover specific reflexive and routine practices and to provide useful cases that signal contributing factors to declaring various identities, including a genderqueer identity—at least in these instances. The sampling procedure can be best described as "stratified purposeful sampling" (Patton 1990, 172–74) to fit the life-history method.

Fourteen individuals (equally divided among "both" and "neither" genderqueer identifying individuals) were selected through the help of contacts associated with various transmasculine communities throughout New England (once again, only two represented examples of "both" and "neither" are discussed in this book). The lead author hired a research assistant who has close contact with transmasculine communities, and he coordinated with the lead author the selection of interviewees. Prior to each interview, the lead author obtained the informed consent of each participant being interviewed. Additionally, the lead author secured a "mix" of interviewees from different family configurations (e.g., adoptive parents versus biological parents). This "maximum-variation" sampling procedure provided a selection of interviewees from a wide range of home life and other background situations. The fourteen life-history case studies—although not a representative sample—reveal the more elusive elements of genderqueer life that are often difficult to capture in quantifiable variables. Each life story deepens and augments our understanding of how the eventual reflexive and routine practices as well as sex, gender, and sexuality change are related to personal life history and thus varieties of identity formations.

The life-history method involved voluntary and confidential one-on-one tape-recorded "informal conversational interviews" (Patton 1990, 280–82). These conversations were completed in two meetings of approximately three hours each. The conversations were fluid, allowing each interviewee to take the lead rather than merely to respond to topical questions. The goal was to grasp each individual's unique viewpoint—his/her/their personal vision of the world. This interview method involved attempting to foster collaboration (rather than hierarchy) in the research process by judiciously engaging each interviewee, "working interactionally to establish the discursive bases from which the respondent can articulate his or her relevant experiences" (Holstein and Gubrium 1995, 47).

This does not mean, however, that the conversations were unstructured. On the contrary, each conversation attempted to unearth the situational interactions and accomplishment of reflexive and routine embodied practices in particular contexts and as related to personal life history. As such, the interviews sought detailed descriptions of reflexive and routine practices, subsequent identities, and accounts of interaction in families, peer/leisure groups, schools, and workplaces. The conversations touched on intimate and sensitive areas of personal life and relationships. Topical examples explored include (1) the interactions among people in each interviewee household as a youth and in the peer/leisure/neighborhood groups of which he/she/they was a member; (2) the power dynamics between male and female adults, between adults and children, among boys, among girls, between boys and girls at school and in peer groups, and between different sexes, genders, and sexualities; (3) any sex, gender, and sexual mentoring/practices during childhood and adolescence; (4) earliest sex, gender, and sexual experiences, feelings, and practices; (5) how and why particular identity formations were constructed in specific contexts; (6) the variable accomplishment together, and thus mutual constitution, of sex, gender, and sexual identities within the same practices; (7) the social processes involved in declaring oneself as gen-derqueer; (8) participation in LGTBQ+ and transmasculine support groups and their social impact; (9) experiences with therapists, surgeons, and the medical community; (10) why and how interviewees came to identify emo-tions, feelings, and practices within particular identities; (11) the genderqueer "coming out" process to others; (12) sexual awakening, how each interviewee managed it, and how images of sexuality were conveyed to each; (13) the meanings and practices of embodied sex, gender, and sexuality throughout their life course and how they were represented to them; (14) the tensions, conflicts, and contradictions in these processes and the way they changed over time; (15) how and why each interviewee experienced sex, gender, and sexual identities as possibly distressing and pleasurable; (16) how practice is embedded in structures and structures are present in practice; and (17) all challenges by family members, teachers, peers, workmates, and others to sex, gender, and sexuality constructions during each life course.

The two interviews discussed and analyzed in this book reveal individual trajectories from family dynamics to university—while simultaneously dem-onstrating the making of these institutions—and confirm the variable accom-plishment together of sex, gender, and sexuality within the same practices that mutually constitutes a particular embodied identity.

Data Analysis

The data analysis for this study had two stages. First, recorded conversations were transcribed, and second, individual case studies were prepared. The analysis here involved open coding, or a line-by-line examination of each transcription, to identify reflexive and routine practices as well as to compare the fourteen life histories (Strauss and Corbin 1998). Consistent with other life-history methodology, the intent here is not simply to present biography but also to explain, in particular, social cognition processes through the life-history data (Connell 1995; Dowsett 1996; Messerschmidt 2000, 2004, 2012, 2016, 2018b).

The goal of this research, then, is to capture the socially cognitive embod-ied experiences of each interviewee in his/her/their own words. By compar-ing individual life stories, we can establish links among the diversity of individuals who identify as genderqueer and whose lives may be quite differ-ent. In other words, we can discover the interconnections among genderqueer identifying individuals as well as the differences between them. Accordingly, life-history methodology helps register aspects of lives that other methodolo-gies render invisible.

The result of this methodology is revealed in the two life stories discussed in "Identity Reminiscences." Both life stories were previously published (see

Messerschmidt 2016), and we reuse the existing data from these two case studies to provide a new conceptualization and analysis not part of the original research.[17] Indeed, the new analysis of previously published interview data adds a novel approach to conceptualizing how reflexive and routine practices mutually, yet variably, constitute a *kaleidoscope* of sex, gender, and sexual identities. Jessie's and Morgan's engagements with different sex, gender, and sexual expressions over the course of their lives help us better understand the changing relationship between routine and reflexive sex, gender, and sexual practices and identities.

We now turn our attention to the life histories of Jessie and Morgan.

NOTES

1. Scholarship on individuals with intersex traits has helped examine the social and cultural construction of sex within the two-sex model. Pioneering work by Alive Dreger (1998), Anne Fausto-Sterling (2000), Suzanne Kessler (2002), Sharon Preves (2004), and Georgiann Davis (2015), for instance, examine the way individuals with intersex traits are treated as "problematic" within the two-sex model—a model that simply cannot acknowledge human diversity.

2. Cynthia Fuchs Epstein (1988) describes a similar process she labels "deceptive distinctions," whereby differences between the sexes are maintained not only by powerful ideologies within biology but also across a range of disciplines.

3. As Kessler and McKenna (1978, 85) describe their research with children on the gender attribution process: "In this system, gender identity is genital identity."

4. Westbrook and Schilt's (2014) theorization of "determining gender" provided new language to more precisely examine the social practices associated with placing others in gender categories. While they understood that this process transpires through interaction, they also note that institutions likewise *determine* gender, yet not all are equally likely to rely on biology-based criteria in making gender attributions.

5. Connell's theorization of "moment of engagement" describes this as "the moment in which the boy takes up the project of hegemonic masculinity as his own" (1995, 122). Here, we use the concept more broadly to examine the ways gendered configurations of identity are similarly "taken up" across the gender binary.

6. Accountability conceived in this way owes a debt to what Garfinkel (1967) refers to as "ethnomethodological" research. To suggest that social interactions require "accountability" in Garfinkel's sense means that social actors share common understandings that allow them to abbreviate their interactions with each other. Garfinkel refers to such instances as "indexical expressions." The point is that accountability not only helps create a sense of ease in social interaction but also holds us hostage to consider how our behavior achieves some level of legibility to those with whom we interact.

7. This is, in part, what Judith Butler intends when distinguishing gender performance from gender as "performative." As Butler writes, "In this sense, gender is not

a performance that a prior subject elects to do, but gender is *performative* in the sense that it constitutes as an effect the very subject it appears to express" (1993b, 314). In "The Future," we critique Butler's perspective, in particular her failure to recognize reflexivity and its relationship with routine practice.

8. While some postmodern and poststructural work is criticized as losing sight of materiality, corporeality, and the like, Connell's theory of gender relations has a useful engagement with bodies and embodiment in her theorization of what she calls the "reproductive arena." For Connell (1987, 1995, 2021), the *reproductive arena* is distinctly different from "a biological base" (2021, 48). The reproductive arena acknowledges reproductive differences between bodies, but rather than suggesting gender stems from reproductive differences, Connell is interested in the ways reproductive differences are brought into social life. For her, the reproductive arena refers to a transforming set of relations whereby ideas about gender become socially and culturally linked to reproductive differences that have no necessary relationship with those differences. Thus, the reproductive arena encompasses distinct features of social life in different societies as belief systems link abstract ideas like *nurturance* or *aggression* with biological or anatomical distinctions to do with sexual reproduction.

9. The ability to understand how relational and discursive structures might, at times, work toward contradictory ends is an important component of understanding durable forms of inequality in social life. For an analogous feature of Connell's theory of gender relations, consider that for Connell (1987, 2004, 2021), there exist four "substructures" of gender relations that she labels power relations, relations of production, relations of cathexis, and emotional relations. Part of what this enables is the possibility that various substructures of gender relations operate to challenge and/ or reproduce gender inequality simultaneously. This theoretical feature helps shape discussions about "progress," "change," and "transformations" in systems of inequality as necessarily more complex than such notions imply.

10. Connell (1987) deals with historically unstable relations of power through her conceptualization of "crisis tendencies" (a concept borrowed from Habermas's analysis of class dynamics and inequalities in late capitalist societies). For Connell, *crisis tendencies* refer to "historical developments that call into question the properties of the gender order as a whole from those that can be contained locally" (1987, 159). Durable forms of social inequality are necessarily unstable, and crisis tendencies is one way Connell's theory anticipates gendered change, challenge, and transformation.

11. This is an important point and something Connell addresses well with her theorization of "emphasized femininity." While few scholars engaging with the notion of "hegemonic masculinity" capture the equal significance of emphasized femininity, Connell's work suggested that hegemonic masculinity is constructed (and must be understood) in relation to emphasized femininities and nonhegemonic masculinities (1987, 183–88).

12. This speaks to a pernicious quality of gender hegemony that Bridges and Pascoe (2018) label "elasticity." As they write, "Privilege works best when it goes unrecognized by those who benefit the most. When the experiences of privilege are fundamentally altered, so too are the 'legitimating stories' that justify systems of gendered power and inequality. . . . [W]e should be careful when assessing whether

these transformations are best understood as challenges to systems of power and inequality or simply shifts in the ways those systems are perpetuated" (Bridges and Pascoe 2018, 269).

13. Jonathan Ned Katz (1990) dates the first known use of the term "heterosexual" to an article published in a medical journal by Dr. James G. Kiernan that was read before Chicago's medical society on March 7, 1892. Kiernan's use of "heterosexual," however, was radically different from its modern usage. For Kiernan, the concept described a mental condition defined by "inclinations to both sexes." Thus, in 1892, "heterosexual" did not refer to individuals with exclusive sexual interest toward members of the "other sex." Interestingly, Dr. Kiernan did not actually have a name for that group.

14. Our use of "mutually constituted" builds on Ken and Helmuth's (2021) intellectual genealogy of the concept across an interdisciplinary collection of feminist research. They suggest that sociologists in particular empirically demonstrate how "the particular dynamics of the constitution of [one identity] category operate to constitute the particular dynamics of the constitution of a [separate] identity category" (Ken and Helmuth 2021, 593). In "Identity Reminiscences," we document empirically this process and build on their call for further specificity and to explicitly demonstrate, rather than simply assert, "mutual constitution."

15. It is important to distinguish between claims regarding mutually constituted identities and intersectionality more broadly. The mutual constitution of identities might best be understood as a component of intersectionality, but not intersectional on its own. Ken and Helmuth (2021) note that scholars sometimes use these terms synonymously, but the mutual constitution of identities differs from interlocking structures of oppression and what Collins (1990) refers to as a "matrix of domination." That identities are mutually constituted may be a justification for the need for intersectional theory and a component of an intersectional perspective and framework. But intersectionality is also more than mutual constitution.

16. Indeed, there is now a defined literature in social psychology explicitly measuring what is sometimes referred to as "masculinity threat," measuring men's responses on a variety of factors to having their "masculine" gender identities experimentally threatened (e.g., Willer et al. 2013).

17. Reusing and reanalyzing qualitative data in the social sciences is fully acceptable, especially since the lead author personally completed the life-history interviews and the data is considered public property because the research was publicly funded (Cossins and Plummer 2018; Heaton 2004).

Identity Reminiscences

"Identity Reminiscences" applies the conceptual framework of sex, gender, and sexuality identities outlined in "Theory and Method"—that includes the coexistence and interdependence of routine and reflexivity—to the life histories of two white young adults from New England (United States)—Jessie and Morgan (both pseudonyms). Jessie and Morgan self-identify as *genderqueer*, but their orientation to gender is different: while Jessie considers her/himself *both* masculine and feminine, Morgan's orientation to gender is as *neither* masculine nor feminine.[1] Although genderqueer people express and understand their identities in diverse ways, they are similar in the sense that their identities are transgressive and thereby challenge hegemonic binary constructions of sex, gender, and sexuality. As such, their genderqueer identities illustrate new nonhegemonic sexes, genders, and sexualities discussed in "Theory and Method." Genderqueer people also differ in how they want to be recognized by others: some accept pronouns compatible with their assigned sex at birth, such as he/him/his, while others adopt nonbinary pronouns, such as they/them/their or ze/zem/zir.[2]

"Identity Reminiscences" analyzes Jessie's and Morgan's life stories *not* as exemplars of becoming genderqueer—such identities are wide ranging and involve numerous ways of embracing this identity—but as simply two individuals (who eventually identify as genderqueer) serving as theoretical case studies demonstrating the symbiotic relationship between reflexivity and routine in the formulation of mutually constituted sex, gender, and sexual identities. "Identity Reminiscences" demonstrates that the *kaleidoscopic* identities Jessie and Morgan occupy over the course of their lives are embedded in changing social contexts, leading, eventually, to the adoption of genderqueer identities.[3] We begin with Jessie.

JESSIE

Jessie, twenty-one years old and a fourth-year undergraduate university student, is tall, of average weight, and wears short (sandy) hair and androgynous clothes and attire. Jessie identifies as genderqueer and defines this identity as "someone who is read and addressed as either male or female, masculine or feminine, or masculine and feminine, depending upon the context." Throughout most, but not all, of her life Jessie used she/her/hers pronouns (and we adopt Jessie's pronouns as she/he accounts for them throughout her/his life story). Jessie's life-history interview allows us to examine the changing and fluid relationship between reflexivity and routine in sex, gender, and sexual practices—and varying identity formations—through home and school settings as we explore her negotiations with the sex, gender, and sexual hegemonic binaries. Our focus here is on how interaction, accountability, and social structures affect reflexive and routine embodied identity practices over Jessie's early life. We begin with family dynamics and progress to other contexts in which Jessie lived, enacted, and frequently changed her/his sexed, gendered, and sexualized identities.

Family Dynamics

Jessie's parents are middle-class professionals with a dual income in a nuclear family household. Jessie spent considerable time with each parent and reflexively adopted from them an appreciation for masculinity and for being her own person. As she recounts, her parents emphasized the importance of practicing masculinity, whether a man or a woman.

> I saw in my mother that she wasn't feminine in the way that society says. The way she handled herself emotionally and her attitude to the world and her personality characteristics all are generally associated with masculinity. She was very confident, courageous, and assertive, and all this has an undertone of masculinity in our culture. And she passed that down to me.

For Jessie, upon reflecting, this form of masculinity became an acceptable intercorporeal practice, a construction solidified routinely by her family's discursive dynamics and social actions. In this instance, reflexivity and routine were separate but intertwined in their relation to masculine accountability, and Jessie describes her mother as embodying this relation.

Despite the primacy of a masculine discursive structure at home, Jessie also described coming to comprehend herself as "a girl." At around age four, Jessie recalls understanding sex and gender as a binary system. The primary occasion for this determination was the birth of her younger brother. One of the first questions Jessie recalls asking her parents was, "Why does he have that thing between his legs, and I don't?" They responded that he has a penis because he is a boy and Jessie does not have one because she is a girl. Jessie recalls reflexively adopting from this conversation a binary conception of sex, comprehending two types of people in the world distinguished by the presence (or absence) of a penis. As Jessie put it, "I'm a girl." This binary conception of two and only two sex categories was a major part of the sex and gender relational and discursive structures in her family's dynamics. Accordingly, the notion that "I'm a girl" remained with Jessie throughout her youth and became an unreflexive routinely embodied sexed practice over time and across contexts. In this instance, reflexivity initiated the adoption of a specific sex category (girl) that was subsequently routinely embraced in terms of bodily display. And not surprisingly, Jessie used she/her/hers pronouns in relation to herself.

Jessie followed the structured discourse at home and adorned her outer body with makeup and dresses, but she would also wear "sporty clothes" when "playing sports, and just do[ing] what boys do, and my parents supported it." Whereas Jessie routinely identified as a girl and assumed feminine bodily display, she understood being masculine as consistent with a "girl" identity as well. Following this, she claimed, "I was taught that I could do anything I want to do," implicitly (and problematically) equating masculinity with agency, yet she never felt pressure to be "completely feminine because my mother didn't succumb to it." Jessie describes this as a form of explicit and implicit permission, took it seriously, and in time came to practice exclusively and routinely her own version of masculinity as pleasurable and with support from her parents and other adult relatives. As a young girl, she concluded that "being a girl" (sex) and "acting masculine" (gender) do not contradict each other and are, in fact, normatively connected, reflexively adopting and embodying what was relationally and discursively structured in her family. Indeed, Jessie's participation in family dynamics involved the active presence of relational and discursive structures in her identity and embodiment, and the active constitution of those structures through the practice of her sex and gender identities.

> My parents taught me that I was a girl, but it was okay for me to act masculine; it was normal to me because my mother was that way. . . . My parents' attitude toward gender was men and women can both do masculine things. My mom did all kinds of masculine things, yet my mom wore makeup and dresses, so I kinda imitated her. So there definitely was room in my house for us women to do masculine things, and that felt good. . . . My mom and I were tomboys at home and we both enjoyed doing masculine things.

Within family dynamics, the primacy of masculinity exists here as the dominant practice and thus discourse. Indeed, what Jessie framed as an incongruence between sex and gender was enjoyable, satisfying, and acceptable in her family. From Jessie's perspective, she routinely accomplished together sex (girl) and gender (masculinity) identities within the same practices, and thus mutually constituted an embodied and accountable tomboy identity at home. That is, within the home setting, Jessie—like her mother—refashioned the hegemonic sex and gender relational and discursive structured binaries by repeatedly practicing "tomboy" as her accountable identity, mutually consti- tuted through both sex and gender identities—girl + masculinity—as indivis- ible features of a seamless whole. This identity was successfully "read" as accountable by others at home, and the body was a crucial component in Jessie's construction of her tomboy identity.

Jessie was also exposed to what she perceived as equal sex and gender relations between her parents—professionals who made major decisions together and neither of whom appeared to exercise more power than the other. Her family embodied what Jessie recognized as egalitarian relational and discursive structures, and in time, Jessie reflexively adopted this as a norma- tive relational arrangement. With Jessie's family, the masculine and two and only two sexes primary discourses did not result in sexed or gendered power relations but were embedded in egalitarian sex and gender relations whereby masculinity was practiced by all, despite the adoption of binary conceptions of sex and gender.[4] At home, Jessie accepted these egalitarian sex and gender relations and describes maintaining self-control over her life. An embodied tomboy identity was accountable at home, and her parents' embodiment and embrace of both reflexive and routine sex/gender practices contributed to her perceptions of an egalitarian relational and discursive structure at home.

Early Schooling

At elementary school, Jessie encountered an unsettling social situation. And her understandings of relational and discursive gender structures were upset. In second grade, Jessie recalled "kids first saying to me, 'You really do x, y, and z [meaning 'boy stuff'] well for being a girl, but you should really do a, b, and c well [meaning 'girl stuff']." While at home Jessie knew she was a girl who was also good at doing "boy stuff," she was often reminded by classmates in elementary and junior high school that because she performed masculine practices at school, she was seen as *different* from other girls. Sex and gender accountability at school was based on a particular intercorporeal understanding of sex and gender relations and discourses that emphasized strict adherence to a binary conception for both. Because of this relational and discursive structure, Jessie experienced tension between her mutually consti- tuted embodied sex and gender identity at school, a tension she describes not experiencing at home. As Jessie said, "At home I wasn't seen as different, but at school I was."

Perhaps unsurprisingly and sadly, Jessie was bullied and subordinated in elementary school for practicing an incongruent tomboy identity primarily by socially dominant popular boys and girls. She describes this as her first contact with public subordination and inequality, signifying the unaccountability among her classmates of the incongruence between her sex and gender display and practices. When asked how this made her feel, she replied:

> I didn't really like the popular girls anyway because they were too feminine acting, they always wore stupid sexy clothes, and they always just talked about boys and the way they looked. So, I just hung out with a few girls like me, other tomboys, and we had fun together.

As the quote indicates, bullying led Jessie to negotiate the in-school hegemonic sex and gender binaries by internally deliberating her response. She reflexively considered the relational and discursive structure of girl identities and the contextually accountable embodiments of feminine identities at school and opted to avoid interrelation and interaction with the "too feminine" dominant girls, associating exclusively with her "other tomboy" friends. Jessie's routine tomboy identity and embodiment motivated her to reflexively connect with other tomboys and to reject the dominant binary relational and discursive structure. And Jessie's friends affirmed her embodied identity as accountable because, within this collective, gender and sex incongruence were seen as an acceptable and enjoyable identity. The collective was an unreflexive intercorporeal social sign for the routine engagement of tomboy sex/gender display and practices. Indeed, reflexive and routine sex/gender practices transpired jointly and in tandem refashioned through incongruence the hegemonic binary relational and discursive social structures at school.

Jessie's response to bullying can also be productively understood as resulting from the symbiotic relationship between reflexive and routine practices. With her in-school tomboy collective, a shared intercorporeal understanding served as a social sign supporting an accountable tomboy identity. Those members never bullied each other and accepted all members of the group, each mutually constituting an incongruent relationship between sex and gender because sex/gender were accomplished together during the same practices. "[W]e all liked doing the same things, like wearing boys' clothes and short hair and playing boys' and girls' sports." In elementary school, Jessie reflexively decided to "fit in" with the other tomboys and to exclusively wear boys' clothes, cut her hair, and participated in the collective practices associated with what Jessie referred to as "boys' stuff." Jessie and her tomboy friends' embodiments were "read" by each other (in addition to other students) as girls who resembled the dominant girls through being independent, confident, and assertive, yet differed in their embodied masculine display, expressions, and practices. Jessie and friends held themselves accountable to their tomboy collective's intercorporeal notions of sex and gender—not the dominant/popular girls' discursive and relational ideals—as they routinely and delightfully embodied tomboy identities.

Nevertheless, Jessie's sex/gender identity and those of her tomboy collective were subordinated relationally and discursively—and thus deemed explicitly *not* accountable—to the sex/gender identity of the dominant/popular girls. As such, Jessie's tomboy collective was marginalized in the clique/in-school social structure. The combined discursive and relational school structure maintained two forms (among others) of embodied sex/gender identities for girls, one dominant and one subordinate. This unequal structure was composed through differing interactional reflexive and routine sexed and gendered practices. Both groups of girls in Jessie's school relationally and discursively reproduced unequal structured relations between them—that is, for the dominant girls, intercorporeal difference involved mutually constituted *congruence* between sex and gender, while the tomboys mutually constituted *incongruence* between sex and gender. To understand Jessie's place in these unequal relations and discourses, it is essential to conceptualize the conjunction of her reflexive, routine, *and* accountable mutually constituted embodied tomboy identity. Accordingly, the structured relations and discourses between the dominant girls and the tomboys are made and remade through the routine identities of each group member, and these same structures are embodied within the routine identities of the dominant girls and tomboys.

Alongside her satisfaction with the tomboy collective, bullying by the dominant boys and girls continued. As a result, Jessie reflexively sought her parents' advice. They counseled Jessie to "ignore the bullies, hang out with people who respect me like my tomboy friends, and they said it was actually beneficial for me to do what I enjoyed, to be myself, to be my own person. So, I did." This example of Jessie's interplay across contexts—home and school—shows how interactions with her parents continued to serve as a social sign that reinforced her reflexive decision to sustain her current group affiliation at school and helped Jessie frame her identity as both pleasurable and accountable to herself and the other tomboys. Jessie continued to use she/her/hers gender pronouns in both settings.

Around age twelve and in junior high school, Jessie noticed that her breasts were changing, and she felt insecure about their size: "My breasts weren't big enough. I would look at other girls who were more developed, and then that would make me feel really self-conscious and that I'm really flat-chested, and so I felt different in a new way now." Here, the embodiment of "other girls" functioned both relationally and discursively and impacted Jessie's sex and gender reflexivity, specifically surrounding her embodiment. Although she continued to routinely identify as a tomboy, Jessie began having serious reflexive thoughts about her embodiment and whether she was a "real girl," due to perceiving a lack of larger breasts. When asked if puberty affected her, Jessie said,

> Yeah, it really did. It changed things because I started to compare myself to other girls and I didn't match up with things like my breast size and it made me feel more like I wasn't one of them. And I was real late in having periods, like four years after my friends did. I could still do the things I always wanted to do like play baseball and rollerblade, and I could still be the independent, strong, and confident tomboy I always was, and I wanted to be. But I did think a lot about being a girl and not looking like a girl and that started to bother me more and more. Like why don't I have breasts like other girls, why don't I have periods, and why do I like masculine stuff? I started to really think about that.

In this situation, reflexivity and unreflexive routine work together, but reflexivity becomes more salient. Jessie continues to practice routinely and mostly unreflexively an embodied tomboy identity yet simultaneously she reflexively questions an aspect of her identity—whether or not she truly is a girl. Reflexive and routine practices occur at the same time because routine practices are fashioned unreflexively, permitting new kinds of attention and reflexive consideration. And we also observe a social sign—her unchanging body in relation to the changing bodies of other girls—challenging her mutually constituted and intercorporeal routine identity as an accountable tomboy.

Jessie describes her body as conveying a new material and discursive message *to her*, and she reflexively responds by negotiating the relational and discursive structured boy-girl binary because her tomboy identity suddenly becomes newly problematic and possibly unaccountable and, thus, unpleasing. Jessie's lack of a changing body now raises questions about her ability to construct a sex categorization as a girl. Her *unchanging* body—through intercorporeal relation to other girls' bodies and the discourse emanating from those bodies—impacted her reflexive practice and worked against her as a fully embodied and accountable girl. Intercorporeal interactions at school indicate to her that particular bodily characteristics are required to be accountable to that categorization. Jessie describes coming to understand more fully her body's contribution to the construction of her accountable tomboy identity. Gendered and sexed discourses and thus meanings of certain bodily developments, such as breasts and menstruation, are expected to be congruent with femaleness, not maleness, and thus became distressing and troublesome. Although Jessie initially pictured herself as a girl, after comparing her body with the changed bodies of other girls at school she describes at this point recognizing new horizons of possibility, recalling beginning to question her identity as "female" or as "a girl." Here we see reflexivity and routine working together through intercorporeal interaction, and the result is that Jessie, not other girls, questions the accountability and therefore reality of her tomboy identity.

Eventually, and following much reflexive deliberation, Jessie concluded that "since I don't have a penis, then I must be a girl. So, I thought I'm a girl, just a different type of girl who doesn't have breasts. But I was still kinda confused." Jessie recounts perceptions of contradictory embodied social signs as coming to be incompatible with her identity as a girl—her tomboy friends never raised the issue. She reflexively resolved this contradiction by deciding that since she does not possess a penis, then she "must be a girl," just a girl "who doesn't have breasts." Through a reading of her body in relation to the bodies of other girls at school, as well as boys' bodies ("I don't have a penis"), Jessie reflexively confirmed her identity as both a girl *and* a tomboy but, in the process, reconstituted her *sex* as a "girl without breasts." Thus, Jessie remained accountable *to herself* as a girl through the above reflexive thoughts. The fact that Jessie had no penis (which is the material and discursive arbiter for sex categorization) became the emblematic social sign for routinely retaining her mutually constituted accountable tomboy identity and participating in the tomboy clique in school. This decision illustrates the salience of reflexivity in negotiating the hegemonic binary structure and its interconnection with Jessie's routinely embodied accountable tomboy identity.

Also, in junior high school Jessie observed classmates engaging in hegemonic heterosexual binary boyfriend/girlfriend relations and heard their "sex talk" about "hugging, kissing, and sex and stuff." Through interaction Jessie learned, as she put it,

> if you were really close to a boy and emotionally intimate with a boy and you are a girl, then you are supposed to be boyfriend and girlfriend. And since all my friends were dating boys then I'm supposed to date boys.

This was Jessie's first contact with the hegemonic heterosexual binary structured discourses and relations at school, and such interaction provided Jessie's initial knowledge about sexuality. She reflexively adopted and activated what was intercorporeally offered and thereby affixed heterosexual practices to her tomboy identity. "I decided to attend school dances because, since I'm a girl, I should find a boyfriend like all the other girls." At this moment, and like her friends in the tomboy collective who endorsed heterosexuality, Jessie reflexively decided to "fit in" and be held accountable to this structural (both relational and discursive) binary heterosexual relationship. Through this process, Jessie reflexively altered the character of her embodied routine tomboy identity—it now mutually constituted sex (girl), gender (masculinity), and sexuality (heterosexuality)—because the three identities were accomplished together through the same practices and became indivisible features of a seamless whole. And now different bodily practices coexisted with this new and different identity; the boy-girl heterosexual structure is present in her practices, and that structure is constituted by her social action. In short, Jessie delightfully constructed and embodied a new "heterosexual tomboy" identity, which her friends "read" as accountable.

Over time, Jessie met and dated several boys. Yet, she found that the interactions were always the same: "We would go to dances together and kiss and go on other dates but then after a short time we'd break up because they'd always say: 'Why can't you be like other girls?' And 'How come you look different and act different from other girls?'" Jessie interpreted such comments to mean: "Why can't you be more sexy in the way you look and act?" She responded: "'I like being me and this *is* me.' Kinda like, 'What you see is what you get.'" Despite finding much pleasure in practicing a tomboy identity, the boys she dated rejected her incongruence and were also aggressive and dominating:

> They just decided everything. When we went out, they decided where we would go and what we would do. And they decided when we would kiss and have sex and stuff. They controlled everything and did it all their way. They always said that's the way it should be, and I didn't want anyone controlling anything about me. They didn't allow me any space to express and assert my desires and needs. In the end and after thinking this through, I would just break up with these guys.

Here, the boys and Jessie routinely construct a hegemonically masculine and emphasized feminine relationship through the practice of sexuality. For a short time, Jessie jointly embodied that unequal relationship: in relation to the boys—and although Jessie was deemed by the boys to be less of a girl than "other girls" at school—she fashioned and embodied a configuration of emphasized femininity. At this juncture, the mutual constitution of heterosexuality with Jessie's tomboy identity momentarily changed her gender practice from "masculine" to "emphasized feminine," demonstrating how the mutual constitution of particular identities can change the meaning of all or specific identities.

Nevertheless, as a routinely practicing feminine participant in this unequal sex, gender, and sexual relationship, Jessie reflexively worked out that she wanted to equally decide what they would and would not do together and to be assertive sexually. But these boys did not allow her that agency. The egalitarian sexual relationship she perceived as modeled by her parents proved challenging to put into an embodied routine practice in junior high school. Jessie reflexively resisted and finally abandoned participation in both hegemonic binary heterosexual relations and hegemonically masculine/ emphasized feminine relations, and continued to embody a routine and mutually constituted tomboy identity (without the heterosexuality part) inasmuch as Jessie now "hated girlie clothes and I just lost interest in guys being attracted to me because what's the point, you know?" Jessie's pleasurable routine practice as a tomboy and adherence to egalitarian gender interactions, discourses, and relations—which carried over from home to peer relations at school—influenced her reflexive resistance to participate in compulsory heterosexual and hegemonic masculine/emphasized feminine relations. Still, although resisting heteronormativity and gender hegemony, Jessie continued to refer to herself with the gendered pronouns of she/her/hers. And given the fact that most of her tomboy friends began to practice heterosexual relations, Jessie maintained occasional reflexive thoughts that her identification as a girl—who abstained from heterosexuality (she perceived her only alternative as being celibate) and unequal gender relations—was now possibly unaccountable, and she began to question the acceptability of practicing a tomboy identity.

High School

When Jessie entered high school at age fifteen, she reflexively understood herself as a girl, "but a different type of girl because I didn't like being with guys and I didn't want to be feminine like most other girls; so, I really saw myself as different." In addition, Jessie reflexively perceived herself as a "different type of girl" because she lived through a body that "doesn't have breasts," which she perceived as unlike other girls at school. Jessie reflexively reconceptualized the meaning of her sex category (and thus embodiment) so as to routinely continue identifying as a tomboy, yet she described starting to feel uncomfortable with this identity—it was somewhat unaccountable *to her*. A new development surfaced in high school, however. During interactions with other students, Jessie heard for the first time comments about same-sex relationships, which, as she claimed,

> started to hit home with me because I felt different from other girls, you know, having small breasts, not having a period until I was sixteen, liking to do guy stuff, and didn't like being with guys, but also I didn't have a penis. So, I was confused to say the least. And then I started to think that hey, maybe I'm a lesbian.

Jessie now reflexively negotiated the structured hegemonic relational and discursive heterosexual-homosexual binary. She began to reflect on the new knowledge regarding same-sex relationships and described beginning to reflect on whether she *was* a lesbian. While her reflexivity during this time was salient, she routinely continued to practice her tomboy identity as an accountable member of her tomboy collective. But after much thought, Jessie decided to talk about it with her mother: "She [mother] said maybe I was a lesbian and what's the big deal, and that I should feel free to explore all sexual options. That if I don't like boys, then that's okay. And she was really understanding about it and said I should just act on my desires. So, I did."

With her mother's support, Jessie reflexively cultivated a close friendship with a teammate on the girls' soccer team. Eventually Jessie became attracted to her teammate "because she was fun to be with," and every day after soccer practice the two walked home together. Their interaction developed into a close relationship. During the walk home one day, they realized that neither liked boys: "She told me she didn't really like dating guys, and then I said, 'I don't either.'" They hugged and kissed and subsequently dated and eventually came out at school as a couple. Through this interaction, as well as the unaccountability of her tomboy identity *to her*, Jessie reflexively decided to shift her identity to include same-sex sexuality—the accomplishment of sex (girl), gender (masculine), and sexual (lesbian) identities in the same practices now mutually constituted what she labeled a "masculine lesbian" identity.

In Jessie's high school, same-sex sexuality was relationally and discursively accepted, and Jessie felt comfortable entering into a same-sex relationship and publicly "coming out" as a lesbian. Thereafter, she spent most of her time with her girlfriend rather than with the tomboy collective, abandoned her tomboy identity, and with much satisfaction and enjoyment routinely began practicing her new accountable masculine lesbian identity. That is, Jessie was now living her body in a new and pleasurable way as she was a practicing member of the hegemonic binary heterosexual/homosexual structure. And Jessie identified a masculine/feminine relationship with her girlfriend:

> I was, vis-à-vis my girlfriend, the assertive and confident one and she was the passive and shy one. My girlfriend looked up to me as her "knight in shining armor" who watched over her. I wasn't domineering at all, just more self-assured than her; kinda "caring self-confidence" is how I describe it—I was her support. So, I liked this relationship because I could be the masculine one; that's what I eventually figured out. And I looked and acted masculine and she looked and acted feminine. So, we were a *normal* couple with female bodies [Jessie's emphasis].

Jessie's new mutually constituted masculine lesbian identity—which differed from her tomboy identity—was successfully "read" by copresent interactants at school who easily visualized each of the sex, gender, and sexual identities within the same practices. And in response to a question about other students recognizing the relationship as a "normal couple," Jessie responded, "Oh yeah, everyone was accepting of it and they saw me as the masculine one and she as the feminine one. Everyone was cool about it." This suggests that same-sex sexual relationships were accountable in Jessie's high school within a hegemonic heterosexual/homosexual binary framework. This further suggests that incongruency among sex, gender, and sexuality were accountable in this setting, at least for same-sex couples who practice hegemonic masculine/feminine relationships. In this sense, Jessie's partnership with her girlfriend satisfied heteronormative criteria; consequently, Jessie routinely and with great pleasure embodied—relationally and discursively—her masculine lesbian identity within hegemonic binary masculine/feminine and heterosexuality/homosexuality structures, and those structures simultaneously are present within her practices. Alongside her new identity, Jessie continued to embrace she/her/hers pronouns for herself, and she viewed this new identity as accountable to herself and others.

Jessie and her girlfriend "had sex" many times but "it was me doing sexual things to her. I was the top and she was the bottom. I was the sexually aggressive one and she was the passive one. I always initiated sex and she followed." Jesse explained that they both would be sexually satisfied, yet it was Jessie's particular sexual practices that accomplished their contentment. Jessie volunteered examples: "Like, I always did the fucking, you know, rubbing my genitals against hers and then we'd both get off. And I'd always go down on her, not her on me." Jessie's bodily practices now have changed to correspond to her new identity. And although these sexual practices are not inherently gendered or hierarchical, Jessie and her girlfriend constructed and enacted them as such:

> I was the guy and she was the girl and I figured out that I became attracted to her because she was very feminine, and I saw myself as masculine. I figured out that I was attracted to her in terms of someone wanting to be taken care of, someone who needed a partner who is strong and takes charge, but again, in a very caring and supportive way. And I wanted to be that strong person and I really enjoyed taking charge. And this confirmed how much being masculine meant to me.

Thus, within both public and sexual settings, Jessie's reflexive negotiation with the two and only two hegemonic gender (masculine/feminine) and sexual (heterosexual/homosexual) relational and discursive binaries resulted in a routinely embodied masculine lesbian identity that was both pleasurable and mutually constituted through sex (girl), gender (masculine), and sexual (lesbian) identities as indivisible features of a seamless whole.

Through internal deliberations about this relationship, Jessie reflexively confirmed the significance of masculinity to her identity. In her private sexual and public nonsexual interactions with her girlfriend, Jessie embodied routinely a benevolently assertive leader and confident protective partner, while her girlfriend routinely was a timid and passive protected follower. Their relationship then constituted gender hegemony in the sense that Jessie practiced hegemonic masculinity and her girlfriend emphasized femininity. And both reflexive and routine embodied practices were involved in Jessie's transitioning from an unaccountable and terribly confusing subordinate tomboy heterosexual identity to an accountable and intensely pleasurable protective masculine lesbian identity within the context of school and in their relationship. Comprehension of Jessie's new identity can be achieved at this stage *only* through understanding the interconnections between, and the mutually constitutive nature of, reflexive *and* routine sex, gender, and sexual practice.

University

During Jessie's first semester at university, she enrolled in an Introduction to Women's and Gender Studies course and "loved it." Asked what she liked about the course, Jessie said:

> I didn't know anything about gender and sexual oppression and never thought about things that way. In high school, my girlfriend and I . . . just saw us as being normal yet different, you know. But then I started understanding about systemic sexism, racism, classism, and homophobia. And this was my first springboard into social justice, you know: "I'm gay; I'm oppressed."

With this new social situation, Jessie established new friendships, and as she put it: "All of a sudden, I had like these major friends who identified as transmen or genderqueer and who were also polyamorous, and all of us would hang out a lot and talk about trans and queer issues." Jessie's new friends emphasized nonbinary sex, gender, and sexual diversity rather than binary dichotomy and reintroduced her to structured egalitarian sex/gender relations and discourses.

Jessie described new forms of interactional accountability as prevailing in this setting, whereby intercorporeal *incongruent diversity* rather than intercorporeal *congruent dichotomy* among sex, gender, and sexual identities was emphasized and respected. Indeed, the hegemonic sex, gender, and sexual relational and discursive structures within this collective were new for Jessie as they diverged significantly from hegemonic binary relations and discourses that existed in all other contexts in which she earlier had participated. And Jessie subsequently reflexively negotiated and embodied the collective discourses, relations, forms of accountability, and reflected on the structured interactions practiced. She came to enjoy and routinely embody them, a development that demonstrates the coexistence of reflexivity and routine, as well as the active presence of structure *in* practice and the active constitution of structure *by* practice.

During this period, Jessie's use of gendered pronouns also eventually shifted to a more fluid oscillation between masculine and feminine pronouns. Jessie did not adopt a set of gender-neutral pronouns (e.g., they, ze) but, instead, resisted a singular linguistic gendering that comes with adopting only binary she/her/hers or he/him/his gendered pronouns (we use Jessie's her/his fluid use of pronouns here). Jessie commented on her/his new group of friends: "Although I was a political science major, I fit in wonderfully with these folks because I was a masculine lesbian and we would have these awesome conversations about ambiguity and feeling in the middle of things, and not fitting into one or the other category completely." A number of Jessie's new friends "identified as transmasculine folks at various stages of transition." Through interactions with this group, Jessie described beginning to reflexively

> question identities and binary thinking, and I was being supported by my new friends and so I thought I should study myself like everyone else. So, I started really thinking about my identity, you know? Like am I butch, trans, or what and how does all this relate to my love of being masculine?

In this setting, the new sex and gender relational and discursive structures influenced Jessie's internal deliberations, practices, embodiments, and identity. Reflexivity became salient as Jessie quickly came to be an accountable member of this new group and began interrogating the routine of her/his current masculine lesbian identity. Through participation in this group and its particular relational and discursive structures, Jessie now had access to information about alternative sex, gender, and sexual identities. Jessie therefore reflexively explored "how I really feel and what my gender identity really means and what sexuality is and isn't." As Jessie elaborated, continuous intercorporeal interactions with her/his new friends and new forms of discursive sex, gender, and sexual knowledge

> led me [Jessie] to think at first about transitioning because I thought about my masculine presentation and stuff like hormones and breast surgery and coming out later. And so, after a lot of conversations with my transmasculine friends and with myself, I decided to start binding and wearing more elaborate male clothes and go out and try to pass as male. I was experimenting to see if I liked it.

Jessie reflexively decided to "try on" or temporarily embody a different mutually constituted sex and gender identity, based on new ideas, discourses, and information learned in this group about binding, packing, breast surgery, and hormones. Initially, Jessie reflexively contemplated constructing embodied binary congruency between sex (male) and gender (masculine)—that is, to "pass as male to see if I wanted to transition." Jessie began to reflexively make sense of diverse identities and experiences in a new context, with new discursive knowledge and a supportive community of creative ways of thinking about and embodying sex and gender identities. Given that Jessie now describes her/his masculinity as seemingly fixed or solid, Jessie reflexively decided to investigate ways of aligning her/his body and sex with her/his masculine identity to see if transitioning would be experienced as sex and gender confirming and pleasurable. Jessie's experiments then involved *attempts* at the mutual constitution of embodied maleness and masculinity— what such a mutual constitution meant and how it felt. In other words, Jessie was in the process of possibly constructing a new mutually constituted sex and gender routine and thereby embodied identity formation.

After carefully assessing various experiments as well as ongoing discussions with her friends, Jessie reflexively decided against binary congruence between sex and gender and chose instead to embody a nonbinary sex and gender mutually constituted fluid identity, which included a political twist:

> I wanted people to question their own understanding of what I am, what my body represents, and you can't just assume I am some particular sex or gender. I connected back to when I was a tomboy and now a lesbian and how I enjoyed being masculine with girlfriends. But I also thought about that I'm female-bodied but also, I've never been a traditional girlie girl. I've always been kinda both—I'm assertive but also very emotional—so I started to see myself in the middle, you know, a combination of masculine and feminine.

For Jessie, interactions with her/his university friends and experiments expressing sex and gender in varied ways resulted in reflexively conceptualizing the meanings of past routines in her/his life, such as being a "tomboy," as well as other life-meaning details, for example, not liking to "be with boys," and why Jessie liked sex and intimacy with feminine women. Jessie concluded that the reason for all of these is

> because I liked *being* masculine. And with my transmasculine friends, I could really express the masculine part of me, but at the same time I'm female-bodied and I always liked my female body even if it was confusing at times. So, for the first time I found the *real me*, and people were accepting the *real me*, which is a female-bodied person who likes masculinity [Jessie's emphasis].

Consideration of both her/his past routine identities that refigured binary relations as well as negotiations with the incongruent diversity embedded in the relational and discursive structures of the transmasculine group impacted Jessie's decision against hegemonic binary congruence. But significantly, the fact that Jessie lived through a female-sexed body and that she/he liked that body motivated Jessie to reflexively decide *not* to transition and instead to identify as "genderqueer," which she/he now claimed to be the "real me." Jessie's body then was a participant in configuring a new nonbinary sex/gender identity, an identity that involved new bodily practices. Jessie's masculine lesbian refashioned binary identity was no longer accountable *to her/him* as Jessie's transmasculine friends emphasized that she/he "could be whatever I want to be" and "could create my own narrative, there was no right or wrong way, it was up to me. So, I decided I'm in between. I decided that genderqueer was the best way to describe my identity. And I can be masculine when I want and feminine when I want."

Jessie's interactions in the close-knit transmasculine group and its relational and discursive structures, as well as past identities that all incorporated a female sexed embodiment, influenced her/him to reflexively become accountable to, and thus to routinely enact, a nonbinary genderqueer identity, which Jessie described as the *"real me."* Jessie subsequently came to routinely mobilize this pleasurable and mutually constituted sex and gender identity. To be sure, Jessie's transmasculine group's discursive emphasis on masculine primacy and shared understanding of diversity in sex/gender/sexual arrangements, as well as Jessie's sexed female body, all served as social signs supporting Jessie's routine participation in sundry sex/gender/sexual doings and ultimately a genderqueer identity. The other members of the transmasculine group simultaneously "read" Jessie as practicing a mutually constituted genderqueer identity, and Jessie and other genderqueer friends would regularly and routinely go out at night in drag in multiple ways:

> It's what we like to do sometimes. And sometimes I'd be totally masculine like put facial hair on, binding and packing, and go out to clubs and parties or just out in it, you know. And then sometimes I'd go out very feminine, lotsa makeup, a long wig, tight top and short skirt, stockings and high heels. But most of the time when we go out, I'm androgynous—I put on the wig and facial hair but no binding or packing, but a tight top, short skirt, and tennis shoes or other combinations. We are genderqueers because we queer gender, we disrupt the normal. It's all about making people question me and themselves. We are gender outlaws; we make people aware that gender is fluid.

As Jessie reflects, they never requested binary or nonbinary pronouns because that would thwart the political purpose of such gender enactments:

"making people question me and themselves." Jessie identified a practicing genderqueer as one who is "read and addressed as either male or female, masculine or feminine, or masculine *and* feminine, depending upon the context." Accordingly, Jessie reflexively alternated among masculine, feminine, and androgynous performances, pronouns, and identities consistent with the particular context, and while these shifts occurred routinely, Jessie described them as accompanied by both reflexivity and a level of intentionality.

One important shift occurred when Jessie worked at her/his part-time job. Interacting outside the transmasculine group, Jessie experienced a new form of accountability at work and new relational and discursive structures, which changed the mutual constitution of her/his sex and gender. Jessie mentioned that when she/he goes to work, she/he wears makeup and fashionable feminine clothing and is recognized as female, "but a very confident and assertive female." In the context of work, then, "I present as feminine, but I'm very self-assured and strong-willed. I'm easily identified as female, and I'm dressed in a fashionably feminine way, but I act like men do. So, I combine masculinity and femininity. This way, people at work see me for who I am, that I'm not just one gender, but both. That's me." At work, then, Jessie reflexively anticipates new forms of accountability and social structures and thereby constructs herself/himself as recognizably feminine—but in ways that Jessie understands as mutually constituted with self-confident, determined, and resolute "masculine" qualities.[5] Jessie assembled routinely and mutually constituted accountable sex (female) and gender (masculine) identities at work that were attended by different embodiments, and in turn her/his practices were part of the workplace relational and discursive social structures.

Jessie practiced a fluid embodied genderqueer identity that was reflexively *and* routinely accountable: "Sometimes I'm masculine, sometimes feminine, but most of the time both." Jessie practiced different mutually constituted combinations of sex and gender embodied incongruency/fluidity as genderqueer, and the particularized embodiment was differently accountable in each setting. And thus, the mutual constitution of sex and gender also asserted incongruency/fluidity within the same practices. Masculinity remained a routine component of Jessie's genderqueer identity but was now only one part of that identity that Jessie reflexively and situationally emphasized or deemphasized in different contexts and at different times. In short, Jessie now transcended, surpassed, and moved beyond a binary conception of sex and gender (except in certain settings, such as the work context) and instead constructed an accountable, confirming, and pleasurable (the "real me") nonbinary genderqueer identity within the transmasculine group that reproduced relational and discursive structures and underlined egalitarian sex/gender diversity.

Jessie also—at the time of the interview—lived with a female-bodied partner in a relationship Jessie considered to be equal in all aspects (financial obligations, household labor, caring for each other), with no sex, gender, or sexual dichotomy as they both routinely embodied sex, gender, and sexuality in different ways, depending on the situation. Sexually and relationally, Jessie and her partner practiced polyamory: "She's my primary partner but we don't believe in marriage and we see other people. But when we are together, we're very egalitarian in terms of giving and receiving." As Jessie further put it:

> We're very balanced regarding sexuality. We're 50/50 regarding top position. Sometimes I'll wear a strap on and sometimes she will. We both give and receive, we both penetrate and receive, and we both equally initiate sex. We play with gender during sex. Sometimes I give her "blow jobs" and sometimes she does it to me. And I go down on her and she does the same to me. We take on masculine and feminine roles depending on how we feel.

This relationship is "skoliosexual" because Jessie and her/his partner are sexually attracted to each other inasmuch as they both practice nonbinary genders, and their sexuality is likewise fluid but also simultaneously reflexive (deciding together what to do) and routine (playing with gender). Jessie reflexively adopted polyamory because it did not lock her/him into any particular form of sexuality:

> I think sex is sex and it's not about a sexual orientation. The things you do during sex can definitely be about particular orientations, such as the actual sexual acts you engage in, but the idea and concept of "having sex" with someone is not.

Jessie's fluid and pleasurable sexuality that included polyamory and skoliosexuality also comprised pansexuality, as she/he recently interacted sexually with "a few male-bodied people," and the sexuality was never "simply penile/vaginal missionary position intercourse. I've done a lot of different things with guys." Jessie provided an example:

> A. During sex with these guys I sometimes present as masculine and sometimes I don't. And when I'm masculine I deliberately ask for male pronouns and so these guys would masculinize me when having sex with me. We engaged in penetration, but then it was always me on top, I was fucking them. You see, sexuality for me is not necessarily about our bodies, our sex, or our orientation because I like a lot of different sex acts with a lot of different people.

> Q. Does having breasts and not having a penis impact your masculinity at all during sexuality?

> A. Not at all because it's not all about being masculine. I can be masculine without having a penis; masculinity is fluid even during sex. Like I just said,

even if a guy penetrates me, I'm controlling the penetration, not him. I'm on top and deciding how that penis is being used—I genderqueer it, I genderqueer sex. And so, I can be masculine but also have a vagina and breasts. That's the whole point, I'm both, not one or the other. Plus, I'm not interested in being male and the breasts and vagina are there and they are very much a part of my sexuality.

Q. Can you give me another example?

A. Yeah, sure. One male-bodied person I had sex with uses male pronouns but identifies as femme, and so I'm really attracted to gender ambiguity and queer people in general. And with him I presented as femme, asked for feminine pronouns, but I also fucked him, and he fucked me. So, I'm most comfortable sexually with people who allow a lot of fluidity in a lot of things and are really comfortable with themselves and comfortable with people who want to be whatever way they want to be. So, we were fluid in our fucking and at the same time we both enjoyed my breasts together and we both enjoyed his cock. So, it's always very fluid and it's always a combination of masculinity and femininity.

In these interactions both reflexive and routine practices transpired simultaneously, combinations of embodied incongruence and fluidity among sex, gender, and sexuality varied, and therefore, the mutual constitution of sex (male and female), gender (masculine, feminine, and androgyny), and sexuality (skoliosexual/polyamory/pansexuality) in the same practices likewise fluctuated. Jessie finished the interview by expressing what masculinity meant to her/him as a routinely practicing egalitarian but fluid nonbinary genderqueer:

Since I'm genderqueer I'm both masculine and feminine and so masculinity is now only *one* piece of my gender, it's no longer *the* piece. So, my masculinity is always associated with my femininity, they always go together: My masculinity is always a tender masculinity that's aggressive but not dominating and overpowering; it's confident but also very respectful, caring, and tender toward others in terms of the way I am. It's other-oriented, meaning I think of other people—I think of how my actions and words may affect other people, so I'm very respectful. But I also value myself in my words and actions in a way that is masculine, such as taking up space and presence in the world. I don't define this in terms of entitlement, but I feel I have a right to be here and when I'm doing something, I have the right to do it. I'm very assertive but I'm also very emotional. But because I'm sensitive to my partner's needs and wants, my masculinity consists of a combination of confidence and caring and entails negotiation not dominance. It always goes together with my femininity.

MORGAN

Morgan is twenty-five years old, an undergraduate university student, petite with short curly dark hair and dressed in androgynous attire. Morgan defined genderqueer as "being gender fluid so that I express many genders in a multifaceted way." During much of Morgan's life, she/he/ze used she/her/hers pronouns, later changed to he/him/his, and eventually adopted ze, zem, and zir. Like Jessie, Morgan's life-history interview allows the examination of the changing and fluid relationship between reflexivity and routine in varying identity formations through home and school settings as we explore Morgan's negotiations with the sex, gender, and sexual hegemonic binaries. The focus is on how interaction, accountability, and social structures affect reflexive and routine practices over Morgan's life. We begin with family dynamics and progress to other contexts in which Morgan lived, enacted, and frequently changed sexed, gendered, and sexualized identities. Similar to our discussion of Jessie, we shift between pronouns consistent with Morgan's various identities over the life course.

Family Dynamics

Morgan grew up in a working-class family, and both parents worked outside the home: her father was a factory worker, and her mother was a receptionist. Morgan was very close with both parents and explained that there was little emphasis on sex or gender difference in her household. Like Jessie, Morgan claimed to have never felt pressured "to act like a girl at home." For example, when the family went camping, "me and my mother always put the tents up and started the fire in the fire pit and my brother and father set up the camp kitchen and actually did most of the cooking."[6] Morgan's chores at home ranged from helping both parents cook and clean up after each meal to taking out the garbage, shoveling snow in the winter, and mowing the lawn in the summer. By engaging in these bodily chores, then, Morgan's practices were reflexively constituted within relational and discursive social structures at home, and those structures were actively present within her in-home routine practices.

Morgan described her childhood family life as "nonviolent, easygoing, and supportive" and talked about not dressing in feminine clothing but rather enjoyed being exclusively "dressed like the boys. My friends were both boys and girls . . . and we all did boy things together." Indeed, and like Jessie's family, one of the dominant discourses emphasized masculinity, and thus doing embodied masculine "boy things" was stressed and solidified routinely by the in-home relational and discursive structures.

Through interaction as a young child, however, Morgan reflexively appropriated the hegemonic sex binary that some people are male and some female and that the distinction between the two is based on bodily difference. As Morgan recalled:

> At around age five or six I had a friend who was a boy and we would compare our bodies, and we discovered our difference—he had a penis and I didn't—and I never really thought about that difference before. So, it became "show me yours and I'll show you mine." We would do it now and then in the basement of my house, and that's how I learned I was a girl.

This bodily comparison became routine for Morgan and led her to reflexively conclude that there are two and only two types of people in the world: those who have a penis (male) and those who do not (female). And this discursive binary sexed distinction became an unreflexive routine embodied practice for Morgan throughout her childhood—she recurrently identified as "a girl." The routine practice Morgan described led her to reflexively consider her sexed identity, which in turn initiated the adoption of a specific sex category (girl) that subsequently was routinely embraced. Morgan actively welcomed a binary conception of sex in which this identity was routinely embodied over time and across contexts; Morgan's body was an active participant in the appropriation of this particular identity. And Morgan used she/her/hers pronouns in relation to herself.

By age ten, similar to Jessie, Morgan began to practice a tomboy identity as both parents supported this sex and gender display and practice. Morgan became an accountable tomboy in the home setting and described her routine tomboy identity as involving pleasurable activities: "just only interested in boys' clothes, never wore dresses, and doing only boy things, like riding bikes with friends, and we'd be gone like all day, playing catch and sports, and even wrestling with guys. I didn't have any interest in girl clothes and what girls do." Within the home setting, it was acceptable for Morgan to prioritize masculinity, and thus, she lived her body in a specific way by reworking the sex and gender hegemonic binaries through routinely and unreflexively accomplishing together sex (girl) and gender (masculinity) identities in the same practices. Such practices mutually constituted a fully embodied and accountable tomboy identity as indivisible features of a seamless whole.

Morgan also mentioned that she always wore a baseball cap to school and finally was told by a teacher that she could not wear it inside the school building. Morgan and her father went to see the principal the next day, and "both of us wore baseball caps during our meeting with him. And my father was so cool—he convinced the principal to allow me to wear my cap in school." Morgan and her father were very close and often went fishing together: he taught her how to ride a bike, they frequently played catch, and they built a tree house together. Both of Morgan's parents supported her tomboy identity; it was a routine and pleasurable embodiment that was seen as accountable at home. When asked if she enjoyed practicing a tomboy identity, Morgan responded: "I did. I knew there was a difference between me and boys, but I never saw it as limiting what I could do. Because my parents were so supportive, I felt I could do anything I wanted and I really loved to do what people called 'boys' stuff,' and it was just more comfortable to wear boys' clothes. So, I just saw the label as indicating who I am." At home, then, Morgan reflexively concluded that "being a girl" and "doing boys' stuff" did not contradict each other, and thereby their collaborative and mutually constituted composition became a routinized, accountable, confirming, and enjoyable tomboy identity.

Morgan's parents embodied relational and discursive social structures emphasizing sex/gender equality and the acceptance of sex and gender incongruent embodiment. And Morgan assumed routinely what was structurally offered and in turn reproduced the social structures through her social action. Morgan conveyed during the interview that at home she could reflexively "choose how to be and to go after it, to be laid back but also stubborn in not letting others push me around, and to be confident in myself." Yet, Morgan's embodied routine and accountable tomboyism at home was different from Jessie's in the sense that Morgan did not construct femininity at all but, rather, eschewed femininity altogether, although she and others recognized her as "a girl." Morgan's tomboy identity was successfully "read" as accountable by others at home, and her body was an integral participant in the construction of her tomboy identity. And like Jessie, Morgan routinely used she/her/hers pronouns within this setting.

Early Schooling

Unlike Jessie, Morgan's participation in elementary and junior high school was not necessarily a disconcerting situation. Following her tomboy identity at home, Morgan reported that, in both elementary and junior high school, she reflexively joined a core pack of girls who were "smart, sporty, and tomboyish" and quite popular because they participated in "all kinds of sports," many of whom were the best players on the various teams. Morgan identified the following cliques in her elementary and junior high schools: "There was the popular crowd, the preppies and us tomboys and guy jocks, there were the emos and the punks, the geeks, like those in band and theatre, and the nerds." Although Morgan and her tomboy friends were popular "because we were the stars on the sports teams," they often criticized the preppy girls for "putting on masks [makeup] and wearing sexy clothes trying to attract boys. We didn't like that; we saw it as stupid." As Morgan described it, there were two competing dominant popular girls' groups at school—the preppies and the tomboys. "We all knew we were different from the preppy girls, but we liked being who we were, and it never bothered us—we saw the preppy girls as the different ones." Morgan found the tomboy identity at school pleasurable, and although she identified the preppy girls and tomboys as "different," she refused the notion that tomboys were somehow subordinate to the preppies— it was the latter who were simply "the different ones." Morgan elaborated on the intercorporeal similarities and differences between the two groups of popular dominant girls:

> I mean for similarities we all played sports and we were all very confident in ourselves, we weren't insecure at all. But the biggest difference was we just looked different than the preppies. Like after practice and games they'd dress all sexy and we wouldn't, and they had longer hair and wore makeup and we didn't. That was the major difference; plus, we were better at sports.

Even though Morgan and her tomboy friends identified as girls, they negotiated the sex and gender structured relational and discursive hegemonic binaries by routinely rejecting the heteronormative preppy-girl femininity and instead embodied masculine display ("boys' clothes") and masculinity practices ("boys' things"). Although the tomboys were "sport stars" and thus members of one of two dominant girl groups in her school, their distinct status relationship with the preppies maintained an unspoken yet discursive designation of them as lesser girls. Morgan's accountable tomboy identity that developed at home was nevertheless easily transposable to the new setting of school, as incongruence had a degree of acceptance in her school. That is, Morgan cherished the fact that she was an accountable and routine member of this dominant group and continued to use she/her/hers gender pronouns throughout elementary and into junior high school. Indeed, her mutually constituted tomboy identity was successfully "read" as such by both the other tomboys and by those Morgan identified as preppies. And the collective of dominant tomboys served as an intercorporeal and institutionalized social sign supporting her routinely embodied tomboy identity, and it held each other accountable to their ongoing mutual constitution of sex (girl) and gender (masculine) identities as indivisible features of a seamless whole. For Morgan, the dominant girls' groups—preppies and tomboys—were constructed through practices that were seen as different in terms of sex/gender styles and prestige within relational and discursive social structures, as well as the active presence of structure embodied in practice and the active constitution of structure by embodied practices.

The competitive relationship between dominant girl groups continued throughout elementary school, yet by the time Morgan was well into junior high school her ongoing interactions (relationally and discursively) suggested that "girls were supposed to be interested in boys. All over school people were talking about boyfriends and girlfriends and who was hooked up with who, even my tomboy friends—everyone was changing. That was the way it was; it was just what girls were expected to do." The intercorporeal inter-action led Morgan, for the first time, to negotiate the hegemonic relational and discursive boy/girl binary prevalent in her school. After numerous inner dialogues particularly surrounding expressing a desire to "fit in" and remain accountable—because she did not want to be the only member of her group who did not change—Morgan reflexively recalled,

> Hey, I'm a girl, right? So maybe I should act like one, act like all the other girls. And so, I started to talk to my tomboy friends about clothes, makeup, growing my hair long, and stuff like that. Plus, we started to talk about boys all the time, and we all started acting heterosexual by showing an interest in boys like "Wow, he sure looks cool." Stuff like that.

When asked if she and her girlfriends were still tomboys, Morgan replied, "Oh yeah, all of us, but we started to have an interest in boys, and we started to talk about fashion stuff, so we all started to change." Her routine tom-boy practices allowed Morgan to reflexively consider the boy/girl binary, and Morgan's sexed body—"I'm a girl, right, so maybe I should act like one"—became a social sign that encouraged reflexively interrogating her tomboy identity. Like Jessie, Morgan's sexual awakening began in junior high school—"we all started acting heterosexual"—as it was here where she also encountered experiencing the in-school hegemonic structure of hetero-sexual binary relations and discourses, and she recalls reflexively deciding to become an active participant within this structure. As a result of ongoing interactions and internal deliberations, Morgan eventually reflexively decides to embody sex and gender differently—in terms of clothing style, makeup, hairstyle, and interest in boys—which resulted in a newly embodied and accountable identity.

What particularly impacted Morgan's reflexivity was her changing body: "My breasts got a lot bigger, I started to have periods, and I started to grow taller and my hips changed." Morgan's body became a social sign that impacted her in a different way than Jessie: Morgan's bodily changes led her to reflexively engage in more numerous and serious inner dialogues about what her reshaped body "meant for me as a girl. I saw all my tomboy friends becoming more sexed in their bodies and more girlie in their presentation, plus my body was really changing, so I thought it was time for me to grow up and be like them and be a real girl too."

Given the changes to her body due to the onset of puberty, and her intercorporeal reading of other girls' bodies, Morgan reflexively determined that

> being a [feminine] girl seemed more important now because my body changed in a very binary way. So, I just started to think that I should be like my friends, and so I began working on creating a very polarized gender presentation. I grew my hair longer and wore more feminine type of clothing and I even started to wear makeup like my friends. . . . I was still involved in sports but after each practice and game, I now started to let my hair down, put on some makeup, and more and more girl type clothes, but I still didn't let people push me around. I went after what I wanted, and I stood my ground. But I looked like all the other girls now. I guess you could say I became a preppy—we all were now!

Morgan reflexively questioned and eventually rejected the accountability of her tomboy identity, and through internal conversations she initiated the adoption of a new routine feminine "preppy-girl" accountable identity—she began to embody the heteronormative relational and discursive structures at school.

Morgan reflexively decided to change her identity and "do the preppy-girl thing," in part, because her girlfriends were also going through embodied sex and gender changes, just as she was. Her transformed body, as Morgan put it, "slapped me in the face." It became a participant in her agency, and thus she reflexively changed her gender identity to fit her feminine sexed body; she now routinely practiced an accountable and embodied preppy femininity. As Morgan shared, she and her formerly tomboy friends "blended in with the preppies," and "since I was full blown into puberty and my body became more sexed, I started to think more about my gender and feminine presentation, and I changed." The gender changes among her tomboy friends and her developing body were both social signs suggesting the unaccountability of her tomboy identity, and Morgan in turn reflexively decided ("I started to think more . . .") to completely abandon that gender identity and instead routinely practice an accountable hegemonic binary preppy-girl femininity ("I changed") that accomplished together sex (girl), gender (feminine), and sexual (heterosexuality) identities within the same embodied practices. Morgan changed from incongruence to congruence and, in the process, actively embodied in-school heteronormative binary relational and discursive structures (two and only two sexes, genders, and sexualities as well as the social conventions defining "being preppy") within her identity and actively constituted those structures through her heteronormative binary identity.

Morgan expressed that she enjoyed entering puberty, found it to be plea-surable, and was "really excited about it because it was fun to dress up and be like my friends." Simultaneously, Morgan developed a sexual attraction toward boys. As she put it:

> I was really psyched about having a developing chest and even to begin to have periods, because I saw this as now meaning that being a girl was more important than before and also that it made me more attractive. I was very good at sports, I had lotsa friends, but I still acted like I always did as a tomboy, you know, going after what I wanted, not letting people decide for me but deciding myself, being stubborn and strong. I for sure looked more feminine on the outside, but I also still acted like I always did, so that never changed.

Morgan now routinely practiced a strong and assertive preppy-girl femininity that corresponded to both her friends and the femininity practiced by preppy girls. She reflexively and routinely constructed and reproduced the three hegemonic binaries—sex (girl), gender (femininity), and sexuality (hetero-sexuality)—she found this preppy-girl feminine identity pleasurable, and she continued to use she/her/hers pronouns.

High School

By the time Morgan was fifteen and in high school, she identified as a "real girl" who routinely enjoyed practicing a localized dominant preppy-girl femi-ninity that established a new kind of congruence among her sex, gender, and sexual practices and identities. Morgan pointed to a few dominant preppy-girl practices: "I had switched from sports to taking ballet lessons, and I started dating boys, and it was all great fun." Morgan's mutually constituted preppy-girl femininity was now significantly different from her previous tom-boy identity. It was in junior high school where Morgan reflexively developed and routinely practiced this new identity and carried it over with her into high school—she was now an accountable feminine preppy girl in high school.

Morgan's relationship with the boys she dated always was close and friendly. Yet, when internally deliberating about these boys, Morgan con-cluded that she "actually enjoyed playing computer games with them more than having sex with them." As Morgan pointed out: "I was excited about having a normal girl's body that made me more attractive. Boys were more interested in me now, and I wanted to experience sexuality with them and like it." During her first few years of high school, then, Morgan saw herself as a "real preppy girl" who was heterosexual and attracted to boys "like all the other girls." Morgan continued to practice stubbornness and determination, "to do my own thing," and all of Morgan's friends maintained similar types of sex/gender/sexual identities. And Morgan and her friends were all now preppies, and she enjoyed a steady supply of attention from boys. Nevertheless, the sexuality with all of these boys "never seemed right. When we had sex, it was like I wasn't being seen. I was being interacted with in a way that didn't seem to fit. I felt like a girl, but that wasn't how I wanted to be interacted with." After much reflexive deliberation, Morgan determined that the main issue was that "they all wanted to feminize me." As Morgan explained:

> I started to think about the way I was touched, the way I was interacted with, that it was them interacting with me, not me interacting with them. And that didn't feel like the whole story to me. I enjoyed being a girl and looking like a girl but if being a girl meant being their object then that really bothered me. So, I broke up with all of them because they just treated me like an object and didn't allow me to decide how I wanted to be touched and interact sexually with them.

Here, Morgan reflexively interrogates the accountability of her binary heterosexual identity *for herself*. The sexual interaction with heterosexual boys involved Morgan being expected to routinely participate in a hegemonically masculine and emphasized feminine relationship through heterosexuality—it involved her first contact with inequality. Morgan describes actively practicing emphasized femininity during sexuality but also quickly questioning such a gendered sexual practice. And like Jessie, after a short time, Morgan reflexively determined that emphasized femininity limited her embodied sexual agency and that it was not pleasurable, and she reflexively decided to end each relationship. And these sexual interactions led Morgan to reject and break from the accountability of these relationships and thus her ongoing integration into the hegemonic heterosexual binary relational and discursive social structure of the school.

Shortly after Morgan stopped having sexual relationships with the heterosexual boys, she began "hanging out" with "a gay guy" she had met in one of her high school classes, and they became "very attracted" to each other. Their attraction developed into a sexual relationship that Morgan described as "awesome." Morgan was asked how their friendship became sexual given that she identified as straight and he identified as gay and why that relationship was awesome. Morgan replied that she reflexively questioned her straight identity—because of the bodily interaction with the heterosexual boys—and "we just really hit it off. We had these great long talks about all kinds of things, and once I just kissed him because I liked him so much, and we both really liked to kiss, so we hugged and kissed some more and then ended up in bed together." Regarding the sexuality, Morgan recounted:

He had only been with guys before, so he treated me like that. Our relationship would be defined by others as heterosexual, but it actually wasn't a heterosexual interaction with a guy. I really wasn't a girl and he didn't see me as a girl. I was the more dominant one. He actually encouraged me to be in charge, and I did. And the way we had intercourse was in the way where he was the receptive one, the energetically receptive partner and I was the energetically dominant partner, even though our anatomy was totally contradictory. And I liked it because he didn't treat me in the way other guys did, and he liked it that way too.

Morgan went on to point out that the sexuality with "the gay guy" was "totally" different from and thus much more enjoyable than her previous sexual relationships because the way the heterosexual boys interacted with her was in a very binary way, whereby "I should be the submissive, feminine, receptive partner. And it totally revolutionized my ideas of how I can interact sexually with someone. I liked the way I felt with this gay guy because I was the more dominant masculine person with him, even though he was the boy and I was the girl. I was penetrating him, so it was my first experience at genderfuck" [meaning, playing with traditional binary notions of gender and sexuality]. Morgan and the gay guy had several similar sexual interactions, and each time Morgan felt her masculinity was further affirmed. Similar to Jessie, Morgan here conflates masculinity with interactional dominance, authority, and power. Nevertheless, Morgan also describes this bodily sexual interaction as pleasurable, confirming, and opening up the possibility of constructing new gender and sexual identities. When asked about the nature of their desire for each other, Morgan responded:

I thought a lot about this, and I figured out that it was because we noticed each other's gender more than we noticed each other's sex and bodies. I was attracted to him because he was beautiful and feminine, and he was attracted to me because I was masculine in my behavior. I was a girl and he was a boy, but we ignored that and just noticed our genders. I looked feminine but it was the sex with the gay guy where I rediscovered my masculinity. During sex with him I could be totally masculine, which I now really enjoyed again, as did he, and I didn't even think about being a girl.

In other words, in their sexual relationship Morgan was seen as delightfully masculine because embodied sex was erased, and it was this erasure that allowed the reflexive and eventual routine linking of her body to masculinity during sexuality. While her reflexivity during this time was salient, Morgan challenged the sex, gender, and sexual binaries by routinely engaging in sexuality with the "gay guy," which nullified sex yet accomplished together gender (masculine) and sexuality (skoliosexual) in the same practices, and thereby Morgan mutually constituted a new and pleasurable embodied "masculine skoliosexual" identity.

During high school, Morgan continued to have inner dialogues about how much she enjoyed the sexual relationship with the gay young man. In particular, it was the fluidity it allowed for her to practice masculinity that she cherished, and that she realized how much she disliked the binary "straight" sexual relationships with the heterosexual boys because she was feminized within those interactions. These internal dialogues led Morgan to likewise question the accountability of her overall binary preppy-girl feminine identity. As Morgan elaborated, "It was the relationship with the heterosexual boys, and my experience with the gay guy, that were the catalysts in making me conscious of how I want to love and be loved, and how I want to touch and be touched and how I don't, and how I want to be in the world." In other words, these two bodily sexual interactions led Morgan to reflexively view her preppy-girl feminine identity as unaccountable, a realization that shaped her future gender and sexual identities that she practiced in high school. Morgan engaged in numerous internal conversations about these two sexual relationships, and she reflexively concluded that "part of my drive toward a more serious masculine gender identity was escapism and part of it was incredibly affirming. And so, I don't see it as a bad thing."

Q. What do you mean by "escapism" and "affirming"?

A. It was escapism in the sense that if I'm not a pretty girl I won't be sexualized in the way the straight guys sexualized me and the gay guy didn't see me as a girl at all.

Q. So you thought if you dressed and acted masculine then you would not be attractive to heterosexual guys?

A. Exactly, that was the escapism part. I hated to be treated that way by those guys and I started to think that my femininity helped that, so I wanted to escape from that. And the affirming part was the sex with the gay guy because it actually empowered me to explore again masculinity as my gender. Sex with him was more than just sex; it was also masculine rediscovery for me. It was cool to see my masculinity affirmed, and I connected it to being a tomboy and how much I really enjoyed that.

Here, Morgan is sketching for us how she reflexively worked out that her sexual interaction with the "gay guy" empowered her to break from, and begin to bodily reject, her routine preppy-girl feminine identity and its accompanying culturally ascendant relational and discursive hegemonic binary social structures at school. Her preppy-girl feminine identity was now deemed unaccountable *to her* as Morgan reflexively is beginning to embrace masculinity once again. Morgan is in the process of reflexively changing her embodied gender and sexual identities that previously centered on being feminine and heterosexual, to viewing masculinity and skoliosexuality as more exclusively *routine*, and in which gender now is primary and sex category secondary. Morgan is not quite there yet, but her reflexive assessment of the sexual relationship with the gay young man strongly motivated her in the direction of constructing a new mutually constituted routine identity.

When Morgan was a senior in high school, the gay young man introduced her to, and she began to "hang out" with, LGBT students "because I just found them to be more interesting. They were smart and artistic, and I liked that. So, I stopped hanging out with my straight friends." As with Jessie, Morgan found that her new friends emphasized intercorporeal *incongruent* nonbinary sex, gender, and sexual diversity rather than intercorporeal *congruent* hegemonic binary dichotomy and, thus, constituted new socially structured relations and discourses. And Morgan noted that through interactions and discussions with members of this LGBT group that they supported her position on "escapism" and "affirming" noted earlier, and she became a routine, embodied, and accountable practicing member of this collective. In other words, the new structured relations and discourses in this collective were now embodied in Morgan's practices, and her practices participated in constituting those structures.

Morgan, however, found herself in a predicament: "I couldn't get out of the binary thought pattern of being a girl, even though my LGBT friends were telling me that if I enjoyed being masculine during sex with the gay guy I must be a dude, and if I was a tomboy and I really liked being masculine, I must be a dude." Morgan continued to reflexively mull over her previous routines and thus engaged in "real intense discussions" with her LGBT friends because they asserted that if Morgan had been a tomboy, if she really enjoyed being a tomboy, and if she liked to be the masculine one during sexuality, then she must be "a dude." These conversations with her LGBT friends created a reflexive quandary for Morgan that centered on her body: "I'm a girl, but my LGBT friends are saying I must be a dude because [of] how much I enjoy being masculine." And it was this dilemma that consumed much of Morgan's internal conversations at this time: "It was being a girl or a dude that kept going over and over in my head again and again that bothered me because at the same time I thought I was a girl but my friends said I must be a dude." Following extensive internal conversations, Morgan determined that

> being called female felt not exactly accurate because I no longer felt like I was a girl. And at the same time, I wanted to stay away from heterosexual guys, and one way to do that was to become male and emphasize my masculinity. But at the same time, I thought, "Well, if I become male and grow up, will I

end up masculine like the straight guys?" So, I had all this stuff going around in my head.

In other words, Morgan's female sexed body was a participant in her reflexivity as she "no longer felt [she] was a girl." But simultaneously Morgan considered that if she transitioned to a male body, then she might "end up" like the "straight guys." Morgan's embodiment impacted her negotiation with the hegemonically *sexed* binary, and as such she faced an extremely complicated and strenuous situation that was difficult to reflexively resolve.

As with Jessie, sexuality had a major impact on Morgan's reflexivity because "a significant part of my gender exploration was the sexuality with the gay guy. It was like I found this very affirming thing, but if it meant developing like the straight guys then it also happens to be something I hate. So, it took me awhile to be comfortable being called 'he,' because 'he' was not a good thing in my mind, you know; 'he' was the straight guys." Morgan explained how this dilemma was resolved:

In the end I decided that I wanted to be more complete. I didn't feel right having a girls' body because it didn't feel complete. And also, I worked out that I will never really be like the straight guys if I transition. So, I decided that I wanted to transition by having breast surgery and start taking hormones, then I want to do it before I go to college so that I have a name and a sex and a gender. I started binding my chest first, I stopped wearing makeup, I shaved my head, and of course just wore boys' clothes. I talked more with my LGBT friends about chest surgery and hormones and the two transguys in the group presented themselves as "someone living the dream" which gave me permission to investigate it more. And I started to think that stuff like binding was just a band-aid solution, not the *real me* because I always had to take off the band-aid. And I thought about how much I enjoyed being a tomboy and really enjoying being masculine and how much I enjoyed my gender presentation during sex with the gay guy, and hated the way I was treated by the straight guys, but I would never be a guy like that, so I decided I wanted a male body.

As a result of Morgan's interaction and conversations with the LGBT group in her high school, as well as her reflexive deliberations about the dilemma noted above, during the summer following high school graduation, Morgan reflexively concluded that her preppy-girl feminine identity was unaccountable *to her* and thus decided to transpose the binary by transitioning to male because that was now viewed as *the* accountable "real me." For Morgan, transitioning to male is about being "more complete" and thus "living the dream"—that is, practicing embodied masculinity. In due course, Morgan was able to receive chest reconstruction surgery, began to take masculinizing hormones, and now commenced using masculine pronouns (which we rely on in this portion Morgan's life as he did in his life-history interview). Morgan's parents and friends all supported his decision, and as Morgan put it, by aligning his body (sex) with masculinity (gender), "I now felt totally complete." Morgan routinely worked to transform his body so that his embodied sex would properly correspond to his masculinity; reflexive and routine practices jointly ensued in this process of attempting to reproduce the hegemonic sex and gender binaries in a way that was completely different from when he practiced preppy-girl femininity. Morgan now was in the process of embodying binary congruence between his sex and gender practices in an inverted manner. His aim was to construct a fully accountable identity that mutually constituted sex (male) and gender (masculinity) identities as indivisible features of a seamless whole.

In this LGBT setting, the new sex, gender, and sexual relational and discursive structures influenced Morgan's internal deliberations, practices, and identity development. Reflexivity quickly became salient as Morgan became an embodied, accountable, and routine member of this group, and he continued questioning the routine of his previous "preppy-girl femininity" sexed and gendered identity. And Morgan's attempt to switch his sexed identity from female to male can only be understood through a conceptualization of the above mutually constitutive nature of reflexive and routine sex, gender, *and* sexual embodied identities. Indeed, it was the "incompleteness" of his female body that Morgan described as his impetus to transition. For Morgan, reflexivity about the body now took on a new significance in the sense that it was essential for him to embody maleness to successfully construct an accountable and mutually constituted binary congruence between sex (male) and gender (masculinity).

University

When Morgan entered university, he considered himself to be "a dude," and he continued hormones for the next three years. Because of the bodily changes, Morgan now was easily recognized socially as male, and he found it pleasurable to embody maleness. As Morgan explained, "I washed dishes as a part-time job while in college and worked with only guys, and not one of them suspected I wasn't male." Asking Morgan what type of masculinity he constructed led to the following dialogue:

A. It was all about being totally stealth—a straight guy who dated women. I wanted to be male in the way masculinity is portrayed in everyday life, I wanted to be a "pop culture male," you know, the everyday guy. And I found that to pass, I had to adopt a certain kind of imagery that people associate with being that everyday male. [*Stealth* means he is not "out" as trans but rather is account-able as cisgender.]

Q. What do you mean by that?

A. Well, I passed as a straight male, and I had all the right mannerisms, my voice had changed, and I would strut around, you know, like young, twenty-year-old guys do, and I talked with guys about sports, girls, and stuff.

Q. So you were completely comfortable with your masculinity?

A. Not totally because I was always afraid other guys would find out that I wasn't totally male. And it bothered me that even though I was easily passing, I still felt I was constructing a feminine maleness.

Q. What do you mean by feminine maleness?

A. If you apply male standards to me, I'm way less masculine than if you apply female standards to me. You know, I was short, didn't have a penis, but still, I did easily pass as male. I was stealth.

Q. So what did you do?

A. I started to get advice from the transguys I knew as a form of "skill share," which was well intentioned. They would suggest what they found helped them pass better and feel more comfortable as a male, like "a good haircut will really help you pass." And it's true. I found that the more mainstream I looked the easier it was to pass and [the] less people would question me.

Q. Did you take any gender studies courses in college?

A. I didn't, but my friends did. My major was biology so not enough time to take other courses.

Q. So did you have trans friends in college?

A. Oh yeah, some of my transmasculine friends from high school and I met a new group of friends as well. All my friends were trans in some way. I completely broke off ties with people I hung with before I transitioned.

Q. And your trans friends taught you how to "pass"?

A. For sure. They taught me all about packing, and even STPs, how to gain more muscle in my upper arms, how to walk like a guy, and where to even put my hands and stuff, like in my pockets!

Following the "pop culture male" discourse, Morgan is attempting to routinely embody what he considers to be the "appropriate" and thus pleasurable masculine demeanor that is mutually constituted with a male body. He is not, however, sufficiently there yet because while publicly constructing a "stealth" masculinity, Morgan simultaneously maintained internal conversations about what he labeled his "feminine maleness"—he did not feel fully "real" and thus accountable as a male. He had not effectively realized routinely the mutual constitution of sex and gender. Yet, through interaction with his trans-masculine friends, Morgan reflexively attempted to learn new bodily skills so as to accomplish together sex (male) and gender (masculinity) in the same practices, and thereby mutually constitute a fully embodied and accountable masculine identity. Morgan also noted that the hormones made him "look more masculine on the outside," and he often decided to "watch my transguy friends in public and learn from them, and I'd practice what they did in front of a mirror at home. And so, all this helped me to more confidently pass as a male." Eventually Morgan successfully and accountably embodied the mutual constitution of sex (male) and gender (masculine) identities as a single whole. And now the active presence of the hegemonic binary sex and gender relational and discursive structures were embodied in Morgan's practices, and Morgan's practices actively constituted those structures.

Intercorporeality is important here as Morgan reflexively decides to read the bodily practices of his transguy friends to help him perfect his own embodied routine male/masculine identity. Morgan informs us as to how reflexive and routine practices operate in tandem. As he routinely improved his embodied sex and gender display and demeanor, he simultaneously engaged in internal conversations involving critiquing and correcting his ability to "pass." Morgan continued on this topic:

> The more I passed on the outside—facial hair, lower voice—and the more I did what the transguys taught me, the less I had to police my presentation. Once my voice dropped and my bone structure changed and my face changed and I had a short beard and I got my demeanor right, people never questioned if I was born female because I more easily passed. So, I became more confident and I now identified as male, and I dated women who identified as straight and who were very feminine. So, I applied cultural concepts in a very binary heterosexual way. And I always did the masculine things our culture says that guys do, I mimicked and mirrored those actions and experiences. The straight women I was with were all traditionally feminine and acted like an accessory to me. They were my ornaments, trimmings to my masculinity, and they would masculinize me and refer to my body in a masculine way. And that was really affirming in my transition, to hear my body referred to in masculine terms and to have beautiful straight women at my side. And I liked being with straight women because sexually they only knew how to be with guys, and so, the way they would touch or talk about my body or interact with me was very much as if I was a guy.

Morgan describes feeling as though he had perfected a completely plea-surable mutually constituted congruence between sex (male) and gender (masculine) within the same practices. He also provides an example of how sex and gender are mutually constituted and thus embodied through routine demeanor. And although Morgan never lived with a straight woman, he did have numerous short-term straight sexual relationships and described his routinized embodied mutual constitution of maleness and masculinity as bolstered and enjoyable through these particular sexual interactions:

A. The sexuality with these straight women was equal as we both were "top" and "bottom"—nobody dominated—and we were equally sexually satisfied, but it was a straight relationship. And that's the way I wanted it because these straight women would refer to my clitoris as "a cock" and the women would give me "blow jobs"—and I would have oral sex with them too! And my cock is large enough now because of the "T" for us to have intercourse. And I would penetrate them, and they would have these great orgasms and that was really affirming because I needed to hear that and perform that way to be comfortable with my sex and gender.

Q. Sexuality became a way to confirm your masculinity?

A. It was one of the ways for sure because I was a stealth dude and the women I had sex with made me feel masculine through and through. But it wasn't the only way. I passed in the everyday world and that was confirming.

Q. But being with feminine straight women was very important to you, right?

A. For sure, because being with feminine straight women who saw me as a man, and as masculine and reflected that back to me was an incredibly necessary part of my transition. And the more I was seen with feminine looking straight women, the easier it was to pass. I was the man, and they were the girl. It was a total transition.

Sexuality with straight women involved the accomplishment together of sex (male), gender (masculinity), and sexual (heterosexuality) identities within the same practices and, thus, mutually constitutes an embodied, accountable, and pleasurable heteromasculine identity. Nevertheless, Morgan did not feel it was consistently a "total transition" with all of the straight women with whom he had sex.

Q. Did all straight women you were with affirm your maleness and masculinity?

A. Not all. Some didn't.

Q. Why not?

A. Mainly because I didn't have a penis.

Q. Can you tell me more about that?

A. Yeah sure, some just wanted more penetration than I could give. They were really nice about it, but we just didn't see each other again. And that did bother me, because when it happened it made me feel less of a man, you know, less masculine. I felt like I couldn't satisfy them, so that hurt.

Q. How did you meet these straight women?

A. We would just meet in a bar or club and then meet again for dinner, see a movie or whatever, and then have sex. It was like normal dating, you know, and we'd do it a couple times and if it didn't work out then we just didn't see each other again and we moved on.

Q. How about the other straight women?

A. They loved me. We would go on fun dates and they liked what I had for a cock, and some weren't that interested in penetration—some just liked me having oral sex with them and they enjoyed giving me blow jobs. Some liked oral sex in combination with penetration. So, it was fine, and I had some long-term relationships with a few of them. But it still was always there in the back of my mind that I didn't have a "real cock," and that always kinda bothered me.

Intercorporeality is important here in the sense that Morgan reads his body in relation to so-called "normal" male bodies. Such a comparison led Morgan to have continual internal conversations about not possessing a "real penis," and that persistently distressed and bothered him—he did not feel he was a fully accountable and a "real" binary male; for him, it was disconfirming and explicitly not pleasurable. Morgan somewhat resolved the issue by routinely engaging in sexual relationships exclusively with straight women who affirmed his mutually constituted heteromasculine maleness. He describes these interactions as affirming his body as male and heteromasculine. Despite that, Morgan experienced sex, gender, and sexual identity insecurity—even with the "affirming women"—because he did not possess a "real penis." In other words, not possessing a "real penis" constituted a challenge to Morgan's identity as mutually constituting a "real" heteromasculine male:

Q. Did not having a penis pose as a challenge to your stealth masculinity.

A. For sure, because some of the straight women I had sex with didn't want to see me again and they were always women who the sex didn't go that great with, and that bothered me because I thought I didn't measure up, you know, like I didn't have a real penis, you know, so that's why the sex didn't go that well.

Q. But many straight women enjoyed sex with you?

A. Oh yeah, it just kinda bothered me, not having a real penis, you know. Like I said, that was always in the back of my mind.

Morgan's life story demonstrates how the body is essential to masculine construction in terms of the binary "two and only two sexes" discourse and its accompanying assertion that "men have penises and women do not"—genitalia is culturally significant for one to accomplish together in the same practice a mutually constituted sex (male), gender (masculine), and sexual (heterosexual) identity. Bodies and their visible parts impact heteronormative recurring identities. To be sure, in *nonsexual* social situations, when Morgan was an accountable and pleasurable "stealth dude," there existed congruence between sex and gender, and he easily "passed." Yet, when in *sexual* social situations with certain straight women he was unaccountable, and incongruence among sex, gender, and sexuality prevailed; only in sexual situations did Morgan's body compromise his performance as a pleasurable "stealth dude." This led Morgan to reflexively question the accountability of his maleness, masculinity, and heterosexuality—he describes his masculine confidence as rather diminished because he was unable to consistently and across contexts and interactions mutually constitute all three identities as "real," and thus reflexivity and routine transpired in combination.

Despite enjoying being a "stealth dude" and having relationships with straight women who affirmed his desired sex, gender, and sexual identity, the issue of "not having a real penis" considerably distressed Morgan, leading him to increasingly engage in inner dialogues about the accountability of his identity and whether or not his body properly "fit" with what he understood to be the binary essentials for maleness. Concurrently, some of the university transguys asked Morgan to share stories, such as "when was the first time I knew I was trans and coming out stories." Morgan's transguy friends gave him advice on how to pass, but "a select few" often questioned him about his past. For example, "they would ask me when I first knew I liked 'male stuff,' like baseball, and when I realized I really liked girls. And I thought—but I didn't tell them—yeah, that's part of it, but I also loved to do ballet, I was psyched about my developing breasts, I really liked being a girl and going through puberty, and I dated boys and had sex with them." In other words, Morgan did not share his internal thoughts about when he "really liked being a girl." In fact, he reflexively realized through his past routine memories that he was learning a new routine "from these transguys to selectively narrate, to pull out the pieces of my history that correspond to being male and leave behind the rest—the female and feminine stuff." Morgan reflexively decided to initially go along with what he labeled the "trans narrative" by routinely emphasizing parts of his history that evidenced a "transguy" sex, gender, and sexual identity while simultaneously eschewing the feminine routines of his past. Here reflexive and routine practices work in partnership, and Morgan's previous feminine routines in his life impacted the present.

Eventually, his feminine past routines internally continued to trouble Morgan. This ongoing reflexivity led him to abandon the accountability of his transition, and he began to construct what for him was rationally a more accountable identity *to him*. As Morgan put it: "I realized that a large part of my history was lost and so I attempted to rediscover those parts I left behind, by looking through family albums and examining pictures of my life as a girl, and I started to take that part of me back." Morgan went on to point out:

> I realized that to be a stealth dude I had to reconstruct my entire childhood in order to have a history that doesn't sound weird when I talk about it. So, when I interacted with a few of the transguys, I couldn't say, "Oh, I did ballet and dated these dudes." I was constructing an entire new history of myself. And part of me now—which is post-dude—is remembering and putting all the pieces together to make one cohesive person that had all these experiences. So, now I'm in a new transition.

Morgan reflexively negotiates the hegemonic sex, gender, and sexual binaries by seriously considering his feminine and girl past; he elects to reject the "trans narrative" and, through that resistance, decides to design a new transition and thus a new embodied identity. That new identity actually was originally validated through conversations, and a sexual relationship, with a transguy friend who decided full transition to male was likewise not for him:

> Well, one night I decided to look at my entire naked body in a full-length mirror, and I didn't really recognize myself. And I said, "Oh shit." And I realized I had gone too far. I saw my face and the top of my body as male, but the bottom part was female because I didn't have a penis. But I was afraid to share this with my trans friends. So, I tried to ignore it as much as I could. And then one of my transguy friends shared his experience with me. He had just come off of hormones because he decided transition was not for him. And we talked a lot about this, and he didn't have a penis either and he like me couldn't afford phalloplasty and then seeing his change and having that permission and that modeling of that experience was so cool. And so, I interpreted this as finally seeing the last piece. And I told him how much I liked our talks and he said he really liked talking with me, and we became very close. And then he and I had a wonderful same-sex sexual experience, because our bodies were the same—we both had chest surgery and took hormones—so we truly were the same sex but not your traditional male or female, but still the same. So it was these thoughts and that sexual experience that led me to think I was genderqueer and not trans.

These conversations and interactions led Morgan to reflexively realize that "I'm not straight because even if I'm attracted to straight women and we interacted as male-female and masculine-feminine, I was not afforded the same permissions as regular straight men." In other words, Morgan came to understand after much reflexivity during and after the above same-sex androgynous romance that my relationship with straight women was more of a genderqueer experience, not a culturally straight relationship. And there was always the risk that the straight women would be with a straight dude, and in that sense our relationship was not straight. Some of the straight women were real nice and didn't seem to care that I didn't have a real penis, but I didn't feel right, you know, it always seemed to go back to that I didn't have a real cock. So, I decided I must be genderqueer, flexible, fluid, nonstraight. And this was the case for both gender and sexuality.

The conversation and sexual experience noted above—accompanied and informed for Morgan by his embodiment—allowed Morgan to reflexively interrogate his transition to male and his routinely embodied masculine stealth identity:

I started questioning the next stage of transition, a hysterectomy and phalloplasty, and I thought how expensive they were and how phalloplasty doesn't usually work and how a hysterectomy will permanently end my chance of transitioning back. Plus, I started thinking about being chemically dependent upon "T" for the rest of my life. And then I got this thought that I may want to have children at some point. And so, I decided I'm not having a hysterectomy because someday I'm going to carry a child, and I then stopped taking hormones.

The disconnect from the "trans narrative" allowed Morgan to "look at my past and revisit pieces that got pushed to the wayside in the hope of expressing this one piece, which happens to be my masculinity. And so, the feminine part of me was lost, and that was a great sadness for me because that important part of me became invisible." Morgan began to reconnect with his past feminine routines, and he asked himself, "What did I like to do as a girl?" After reflexively thinking about this question, Morgan realized that much of what he framed as his "real" identity had been erased:

I was on hormones for three years, and I saw it as giving up a part of myself to adhere to the script. So, I started to deconstruct my history and rediscover my feminine past. And I realized how much I didn't like being a stealth dude just as I didn't like being a stealth chick from thirteen to seventeen. So, it was about going back in my history and finding the pieces that made up the whole story. It was like opening a treasure chest that I locked away. All the answers are in that chest that holds the other parts of myself. So, it's a whole new transition and coming out process by embracing parts of me that I haven't had in a long time.

Morgan moved beyond the binaries and constructed an identity that now felt more accountable and pleasurable *to himself* because it mutually constituted "all traits of gender and it's not so much a matter of breaking down specific behaviors as looking at feelings that generate behaviors. I'm neither masculine nor feminine so I don't pass as anything, I don't hype up on one side or the other—I have synthesized everything, and I always use, and ask other people to use, gender-neutral pronouns," in particular "ze," "zem," and "zir" (which we now rely on to describe Morgan). Morgan went on to point out that ze does not reflexively "try to act gendered in any specific way, and others have a hard time reading me as either male or female. People are confused all the time." Morgan stated that people have a hard time reading zem because "I have so many bodies and so many past experiences all wrapped into one—a tomboy, a straight female-bodied person, a masculine female-bodied male, a female-to-male transman, and a genderqueer person—which is a very different gender than being born female and always being female and acting feminine."

Morgan now reflexively and routinely transcended and surpassed binary conceptions of sex and gender and ze explained zir's "genderqueer" identity in the following way: "It's when I rediscovered my feminine past, but when I did that, it's not really going back to femininity as it is going forward to something new. It's like I'm queering queer! So, I feel and act many genders based on this history of different bodies and genders. And if I'm many genders then I'm neither masculine nor feminine." Morgan offered this example: "If I'm in a gay bar, some guys will read me as an effeminate guy, and others will read me as a transwoman, and dykes will read me as a transguy or as a butch dyke. I have a lot of different genders just standing there having a drink. I encompass so much, but I'm very fixed in who I am." Morgan's genderqueer identity was thus constituted as neither masculine nor feminine and became a new accountable and pleasurable identity for Morgan that was routinized and mutually constituted by sex (androgynous), gender (maxigender), and sexual (skoliosexual/pansexual) identities within the same practices and as indivisible features of a seamless whole. Morgan's body and identity now corresponded to each other.

At the time of the interview, Morgan was in a relationship with "a female-bodied person and we both are pansexual. We are fluid in our sexuality as sometimes I'm the dominant one, the more masculine, and sometimes she is." Morgan went on to state that "we change roles—our sex is up, down, and all over bodies. It's always changing. We've engaged in every sexual position in the book, and then some. And now that I'm genderqueer, it doesn't actually matter what my body looks like. My body is in between."

Q. So your body now fits well with your genderqueer identity?

A. Yeah, for sure. I don't have a male or a female body, and that's what fits me . . . I'm neither.

Morgan created a new sex (androgynous) and gender (maxigender), and like Jessie, sexuality now is simultaneously reflexive (fluid) and routine (skoliosexual/pansexual). Morgan routinely practices a genderqueer identity because "being born female gave me a certain set of experiences, and then transitioning to male gave me more experiences, and then adding back in my femaleness gave me kind of a postmodern gender transition. An identity implies experience, and really, I've had far more experiences than one identity can encompass. So yeah, I'm genderqueer because my identity expresses many genders in a multifaceted way."

Morgan finished the interview by explaining how masculinity fits into zir's genderqueer identity:

> Like I said earlier, I don't attempt to pass or act in any special gender way, but some people read me as a straight masculine guy, some as a feminine guy, some as a transman or transwoman, and some as a masculine female. It is difficult to categorize me because I entail so many genders. Masculinity is there if you want to see it, but so are many other genders. You can't say I'm just one gender. It is kind of like the color white, which is really the full spectrum of colors, even though it would be identified as the absence of color. That's what I mean. So, if you were to highlight and look at part of that spectrum, you could pull out the red value, or the blue value, or the green value, in full spectrum light, but to the naked eye it just seems to have nothing. So, if you wanted to look at the masculine part of my identity, you could find it, but it's together with other parts in a space that is usually seen as nothing, like the color white.

We now turn to "The Future" and conclude the book by discussing what we learn about reflexive and routine practices from Jessie's and Morgan's life stories and their kaleidoscopic mutually constituted and embodied sex, gender, and sexual identities.

NOTES

1. Orientations to genderqueer identities as either both masculine *and* feminine or neither masculine *nor* feminine represent a powerful illustration of the fact that masculinity and femininity are not productively understood as polar opposites on a linear continuum. We address this more completely in ""The Future," but we bring it up here as something to consider as we present the life histories of Jessie and Morgan.

2. We are careful to utilize the pronouns Jessie and Morgan used to describe themselves throughout each life-history interview. At different stages of their lives, they adopted different pronouns, and we oscillate between the pronouns each of them used to describe themselves. This reflects their own lived experiences and is consistent with research arguing that such a decision has political implications in challenging dominant/dominating sex, gender, and sexual norms in addition to incorporating new

sex/gender/sexual formations, categories, and identities (e.g., Saguy and Williams 2022).

3. It is more common to use the language of identity "projects" and "formations" in scholarship on race and ethnicity—in part due to Omi and Winant's (1994) racial formation theory. This language is helpful as it articulates identities as "ongoing accomplishments" to borrow Garfinkel's (1967) phrase. Connell (2021, 102–6) also uses this language as it describes what Bridges and Pascoe (2018) term the "elasticity of gender hegemony" in connecting with Connell's theory. We conceptualize "identity" and "identity formation" as fluid and unreflectively routine sex, gender, and sexual practices.

4. It is important to acknowledge that the status and value attributed to masculinity were present in Jessie's (and as noted later, for Morgan) description of her family's dynamics. This form of androcentrism simply allowed equal access to masculinity, but the status relations between masculinity and femininity are—as Jessie describes it here—present within her family as well.

5. Context plays an important role in understandings and enactments of sex, gender, and sexual identities (e.g., Bridges 2009). Context is an integral component of not only in how different individuals, groups, and institutions make sense of sexed, gendered, and sexual enactments and identities but also in terms of how those practices are afforded status. Jessie is not unique in experiencing this at work, but Jessie's experience illustrates this larger dynamic.

6. It is interesting to note how Morgan genders activities in this quote. While "cooking" is attributed a "feminine" meaning in Morgan's summary, it is also true that we often fail to appreciate how the gender binary fails to structure social life as much as discourses of the gender binary suggest. One of the ways this contradiction is managed is through an incredible array of exceptions to gender binary "rules." Although cooking may be popularly understood as a "feminine" activity, cooking professionally is culturally consistent with masculinity in many societies, as is cooking outdoors.

The Future

The interview data in "Identity Reminiscences" yield compelling findings that suggest future research directions for sex, gender, and sexuality scholars. We conclude this work with a summary of the key findings and provide suggestions for prospective and subsequent scholarship. Before proceeding, we reiterate that Jessie's and Morgan's life stories must *not* be viewed as exemplars or typical examples of either becoming genderqueer or of genderqueer experiences—such identities are wide ranging and involve numerous ways of embracing this identity. Rather, we rely on these two life histories as theoretical case studies that enable us to examine and demonstrate the symbiotic relationship between reflexivity and routine in the formulation of mutually (yet variably) constituted sex, gender, and sexual identities.

The two life histories reveal how sex, gender, and sexual identities are products of both reflexive and routine social action. They are *routine* in being accomplished without internal due deliberation and *reflexive* in entailing evaluative internal reflection. The case studies specifically advance gender theory by demonstrating reflexive and routine processes as both interdependent and symbiotic. They further demonstrate that sex, gender, and sexual identities are situationally shaped, are subject to interactional accountability, and involve both the active presence of structure in practice and the active constitution of structure by practice. Relational and discursive structures do not function through direct manipulation but, rather, are embodied within distinct identities, and in unison, those identities compose particular social structures. The case studies reveal the stages in their lives that Jessie and Morgan experienced and the kaleidoscope of sex, gender, and sexual identities from their childhood into adulthood. Jessie's and Morgan's life stories are constituted by a succession of *accountable* sex, gender, and sexual identities that change as their sex, gender, and sexual practices developed and transformed over time and by context.

Over their life course, Jessie and Morgan behaved in both routine and reflexive ways, and their routine and reflexive enactments of sex, gender, and sexual identities variably yet mutually embodied each other. Jessie and Morgan were active participants in a variety of social interactions and relational and discursive social structures embedded in a series of social settings, and thereby changed their reflexive and routinely accountable sex, gender, and sexual identities. In turn, they each describe instances of reflexively disassociating with particular structures, which discontinued specific identity formations. Jessie and Morgan reflexively negotiated with various individuals, groups, and contexts, and each facilitated the appropriation of diverse understandings of sex, gender, and sexuality. Jessie's and Morgan's morphing identity formations were thus reflexively and routinely accountable to the expectations of those same individuals, groups, and social structured contexts.

Their life histories reveal a fluidity of sex, gender, and sexual identities whereby they routinely practiced distinct sex, gender, and sexual constructions that corresponded to specific social contexts. Within and across settings, Jessie and Morgan mobilized varying sex, gender, and sexual practices with accountable consistency, enabling the routine embodiment of differing sex, gender, and sexual identities. Jessie and Morgan described often knowing intuitively what to do in a particular situation—without reflexive deliberation—because of particularized interactional accountability and contextualized social signs embedded in structured sex, gender, and sexual relations and discourses. Their life-history accounts reveal the value of a truly sociological conceptualization of routine behavior, and in the dynamics of Jessie's and Morgan's life histories, reflexivity was intricately intertwined with routine sex, gender, and sexual identities. Reflexive and routine practices appeared in each setting as differing forms of a coexisting symbiotic collaboration that shaped Jessie's and Morgan's sexed, gendered, and sexualized social actions. What we "see" in Jessie's and Morgan's accounts is how reflexive and routine sexed, gendered, and sexual practices materialize jointly, linked to fluid and shifting identity formations in ways that privilege neither. We also "see" how they were situationally shaped by the diverse social structural contexts in which Jessie and Morgan participated.

These two case studies demonstrate how, at each major juncture, Jessie and Morgan were both a *product and a producer* of situationally constituted interaction, as well as sex, gender, and sexual accountability and social structures. Similarly, specific sex, gender, and sexual routines and reflexive practices were products of situational interaction, accountability, and social structures. Neither routine *nor* reflexivity occurred in a social vacuum. Both were situated, necessitating attention to the contextual social conditions in which they were reflexively and routinely accomplished.

In short, this book demonstrates the significance of conceptualizing how reflexivity and routine are more symbiotic than has been generally acknowledged. We substantiate this claim by examining the ways reflexivity and routine collaboratively shaped sex, gender, and sexual accountable identities in Jessie's and Morgan's lives without arbitrarily privileging either. We demonstrate that such processes are extensively in play during daily interaction and that the behaviors and identities that all of us construct can be understood only through a perspective that appreciates how reflexive and routine sexed, gendered, and sexual practices are informed by situationally constituted interaction, accountability, and social structures (both relational and discursive). The content of this book then suggests that it would be invaluable for scholars to further investigate the symbiotic relationship between reflexive and routine practices because such a perspective will enhance our understanding of how actors, individually and in groups, socially produce and resist sexed, gendered, and sexual identities, accountability pressures, and social structural dynamics.

Jessie's and Morgan's life histories in particular catalog a variety of ways reflexive and routine practices are symbiotically intertwined. Each life history recorded numerous examples of reflexive and routine practices being separate but interwoven, such as when Jessie reflexively imitated the masculinity of her/his mother, which she/he subsequently solidified as a routine gender practice. In this instance, reflexivity and routine are distinct but overlapping. The life stories documented how reflexivity and routine transpire jointly, such as when Jessie reflexively avoided interaction with the bullying dominant girls in school and opted to associate exclusively with her/his tomboy friends. In this example, social interaction—bullying—led to reflexivity while Jessie concurrently and routinely carried on her/his tomboy identity. Reflexive and routine practices then often transpire in tandem. This example also indicates how routine practices enable one to simultaneously attend to reflexivity by providing the cognitive space to do so.

A separate instance of this occurred when Morgan routinely practiced a tomboy identity yet at the same time reflexively elected to converse with zir friends about changing clothing styles, makeup, and boys. In other words, while routinely performing a tomboy identity, Morgan reflexively began to question the authenticity of that identity. Once again, the unreflexive nature of routine practices clears the path for the simultaneous participation in reflexivity. The two life stories additionally revealed how routine practices can initiate reflexivity, which in turn leads to a new routine identity. For example, Morgan's "show me yours and I'll show you mine" routine practice led to reflexive deliberating about zir sexed identity, which successively initiated the adoption of a "girl" sex category that was subsequently routinely embraced.

Jessie and Morgan furthermore furnished numerous examples of how reflexivity can initiate change and thus the adoption of new routine gender practice. For example, Morgan reflexively decided to change zir identity and engage in preppy-girl femininity, which permitted zir gender identity to now routinely "fit" with zir new feminine sexed body. And Jessie reflexively embraced heterosexuality and routinely, albeit rather briefly, affixed heterosexual practices to her/his routine tomboy identity. These examples are a handful of many instances that illustrate the different ways reflexive and routine practices are symbiotically connected, and it would be helpful if future researchers continued to investigate such variance.

The life-history data build on numerous aspects of Connell's (1987) sociological theory of gender outlined in "The Past." First, Connell emphasizes a dynamic relationship between structure and practice, so that within all gender regimes, the qualities that constitute gender identities are embodied in and through routine practices whereby such regimes are structured. Throughout their life stories, Jessie and Morgan identified numerous gender regimes—the family, elementary school and junior high, high school, and finally the universities they attended. In each of these gender regimes, they identified relational and discursive structures, such as the hegemonic binaries and their accompanying discourses of two and only two sexes, genders, and sexualities, as well as Jessie's and Morgan's varying sex, gender, and sexual identities that constituted those structures. To be sure, what we "see" through the kaleidoscopic identities formulated by Jessie and Morgan is both the active presence of these structures in their identities and the active constitution of the structures by those identities. Jessie and Morgan embodied structure through their identities; they lived and constituted structure via social action. Depending upon the context, Jessie and Morgan variably embodied different constellations of sex, gender, and sexual identities. For example, Jessie's sex/gender identity and those of her/his tomboy collective in early schooling were subordinated relationally and discursively—and thus deemed unaccountable—to the sex/gender identity of the dominant popular girls' group. Jessie's tomboy collective was marginalized in the clique in-school relational and discursive social structures. These unequal structures were composed through differing interactional reflexive and routine sexed and gendered practices. Both groups of girls relationally and discursively reproduced an unequal structured relationship between them through their embodied social action. Accordingly, the relational and discursive unequal relationships between the dominant popular girls and the subordinated tomboys are made and remade through the routine identities of each group member, and the relational and discursive social structures are embodied within the routine identities of the differing groups of girls. Indeed, this notion that identities are the matter of structures, and structures are constituted by identities, was identified throughout *all* the sex, gender, and sexual regimes in which both Jessie and Morgan participated.

Second, Connell (1987) argues that since humans engage in reflexivity, they have the capacity to "turn against" and, thus, disassociate from particular structures. We identified numerous examples of just such disassociations in the life histories of both Jessie and Morgan, such as when they both deter-mined that their sexual experiences with the heterosexual boys led them to reflexively end each relationship. Both Jessie and Morgan resisted, turned against, and disassociated from their (at the time) routine heterosexual identi-ties and thus integration within the hegemonic binary heterosexual relational and discursive social structures of the school.

Third, the new conceptual framework emphasized in this book further develops Connell's notion of "choice" and "routine," both of which were theoretically underdeveloped in her theory of gender. Instead of "choice," we follow Archer (2007) and use the term "reflexivity" in reference to the capac-ity of individuals to engage in internal conversations about particular social experiences and then decide how to respond appropriately. People construct a dialogic interaction with themselves that involves internally mulling over specific social events and interactions, considering the emotional valence of such circumstances, prioritizing what matters most, and ultimately planning, deciding, and designing a response. And we document in careful detail the ways reflexivity is a major part of the everyday lives of Jessie and Morgan.

Regarding routine, Connell never used this term explicitly, but rather sim-ply noted that certain consistent and regular gender practices over time are "configured" as a "project" and thus embedded in the structures constituting gender regimes, such as hegemonic masculinity and emphasized femininity. We elaborate on this conception by constructing a sociological understanding of routine focusing on when certain sex, gender, and sexual practices occur with sufficient consistency; it is at that point that they become disciplined, accountable, and embodied identities that are practiced routinely. Sex, gen-der, and sexual routine are necessarily influenced by prior practice, and when such practices are contextually accountable, they are likely to be repeated unreflexively as identities. To understand sex, gender, and sexuality as identi-ties suggests that much sex, gender, and sexual routines are agentic; they are conscious—yet unreflexive or acting without internal deliberation about and attention to a specific practice—self-activating practices that are continuous through time and space. And like reflexivity, we also documented the ways such routine was a major part of the everyday lives of Jessie and Morgan.

Fourth, our data also support Connell's (2002, 136–41) notion that sex, gender, and sexual identities are sources of pleasure, enjoyment, and rec-ognition as well as sources of inequality, injustice, and harm. For example, embodying both masculine display ("boys' clothes") and masculine practices ("boy stuff") while identifying as a girl, Jessie and Morgan proclaim for oth-ers (family members and students) the pleasure and enjoyment they derive from doing "tomboy." Nevertheless, each simultaneously experienced dif-ferent types of inequalities as tomboys: Jessie was bullied and subordinated by the popular boys and girls in elementary school for being a tomboy, and although Morgan never mentioned similar experiences, ze does allude to the well-established status differences between the heteronormative preppies and zir tomboy collective, even though the latter were "sports stars." In both cases, then, their position in the in-school clique student structure constructed Jessie and Morgan as lesser girls in different ways because of their masculine display and practices.

Regarding heterosexuality, in junior high school Jessie delighted in embodying a new "heterosexual tomboy" identity but quickly realized that the boys she/he dated consistently rejected her/his sex/gender incongruence and were also aggressive and dominating toward her/him. This juxtaposition offers one illustration of the pleasure and pain that are integral (and sometimes overlapping) components of gender relations. The result was the construction of unequal sex/gender relations during dating. And rather than constructing a heterosexual tomboy identity, Morgan eventually repudiated zir tomboy identity altogether. Once ze entered puberty and zir body "became more sexed," in high school Morgan found pleasure in adopting and practicing a preppy-girl femininity, which included dating boys ("it was all great fun"). Morgan was excited about having a body that was attractive to boys, and ze looked forward to experiencing heterosexuality. Yet, like Jessie, Morgan eventually found sexuality with heterosexual boys to be detrimental because "it was them interacting with me, not me interacting with them." The result was similar to Jessie: the interaction constructed unequal sex/gender relations during sexuality.

The life-history data provide other examples as well. For instance, when Jessie was in high school, she/he began to practice—with much satisfaction and enjoyment—a "masculine lesbian" identity; however, while involved in a masculine/feminine relationship with her/his girlfriend, Jessie was the "assertive and confident one," and her/his girlfriend was the "passive and shy one." Indeed, their relationship constituted a new form of unequal gender relations: Jessie practiced hegemonic masculinity, and her girlfriend emphasized femininity. In contrast to this, while at university Morgan experienced much pleasure in constructing a "stealth dude" masculine identity in nonsexual social situations; however, given that Morgan did not possess a "real penis," in certain sexual situations ze perceived zir masculinity and heterosexuality as challenged, and ze experienced an emotional inequality with assumed "real" heteronormative men.

In all of these examples, both Jessie and Morgan experience *pleasure* and *inequality* in different ways, yet they reflexively and readily fashion each identity and at once cherished and rejoiced in doing so. Arguably, the vast majority of the kaleidoscopic identities practiced by Jessie and Morgan were experienced as gratifying, meaningful, and pleasurable—both were deeply attached and devoted to most of the identities they practiced. Once at university, however, Jessie and Morgan commenced a search for a more suitable identity. And it was the eventual assumption of a "both" (Jessie) and "neither" (Morgan) genderqueer identity whereby they experienced the most pleasure throughout their lives: Jessie found it especially satisfying to combine embodied incongruence and fluidity among sex, gender, and sexuality and, therefore, to constitute routinely and mutually sex (male and female), gender (masculine, feminine, and androgyny), and sexuality (skoliosexual/polyamory/pansexuality) in the same practices. And Morgan was delighted about practicing routinized and mutually constituted sex (androgynous), gender (maxigender), and sexual (skoliosexual/pansexual) identities within the same practices. Indeed, their genderqueer identities were seemingly much more thoroughly experienced and intensely fulfilling than all previous identities.

Finally, Connell went beyond solely a conceptualization of gender, evident in her close attention to the mutual constitution of gender, class, and sexual relations. Following in the footsteps of Connell and others (e.g., Hames-Garcia 2011; Ken 2010; Ken and Helmuth 2021; Tapley 2013), we further develop the idea of "mutual constitution" as occurring when two or more sex, gender, race, class, age, sexuality, and nationality identities are accomplished together through the same practice, and their joint configuration materializes a particular embodied identity. Ken (2010; Ken and Helmuth 2021) has argued that specific identities *depend* upon each other and that such dependence may be temporary or long lasting. Although we agree with this perspective, the life-history data we present here demonstrate that this variable reliance upon each other is mutually constituted within the same practices. Here, we have exclusively concentrated on sex, gender, and sexuality, and when any mixture of these three identities are accomplished together through the same practice, their collaborative composition forms a specific embodied identity. For example, within particular contexts—such as the family and elementary and junior high school—for both Jessie and Morgan the accomplishment together of sex (girl) and gender (masculinity) identities within the same practices both depend upon each other and, in conjunction, mutually constituted embodied "tomboy" configurations of identity. And copresent interactants were able to simultaneously "see" both *girl* and *masculinity* within the same practices and thus successfully "read" their identities as "tomboy." In other words, the mutual constitution of sex and gender identities in the same practices enables—or makes possible—the actuation of a new and particularized identity, which others recognize as intelligibly accountable (or not). And throughout their life stories, both Jessie and Morgan personified their various identities in concert, they were produced alongside each other as dependent, yet indivisible features of a seamless whole. All of this elaboration of Connell's perspective would greatly benefit from future research and further explanation.

The new conceptualization and analysis developed herein incorporates and adds to certain aspects of West and Zimmerman's (1987) "doing gender" perspective, in particular the salience of interactional accountability to sex, gender, and sexual identities (see Hollander 2018). The evidence clearly shows how, through reflexivity, social actors question and sometimes distance and separate themselves from some accountability structures, clearing paths for improvisation and innovation. In other words, reflexivity mediates social conditions, and individuals may then subsequently analyze, investigate, and/or resist (within specific contexts) interactional accountability and social structures. Interactional accountability and relational and discursive social structures *dragoon* but do not *dictate* social action. This perspective on *reflexive mediation* is theoretically absent in the "doing gender" perspective but is central to the analysis in this book, and future research on reflexive mediation would be extremely beneficial.

West and Zimmerman (1987, 126) mention "routine" in their definition of gender as "a routine, methodical and recurring accomplishment," but they do not further analyze how routine specifically is related to sex, gender, and reflexivity, nor do they provide a comprehensive understanding of routine practice. The conceptualization in this book is a unique sociological perspective on routine sex, gender, and sexual practices as disciplined embodiments that construct particular identities. Sex, gender, and sexuality are often routinely reiterated unreflexively, although consciously, because reflexive and routine practices are interconnected through interactional accountability and social signs. Routine social action is always agentic because it is reflexively accessible. Alongside work like Westbrook and Schilt's (2014) theorization of "determining gender," the perspective in this book builds on feminist sex, gender, and sexuality scholarship that expands the "doing gender" perspective and framework. It demonstrates how sexed, gendered, and sexual practices and identities (across varying contexts) are constituted by the coexistence of, and interplay between, reflexive and routine social actions whose combination represents structured *and* agentic responses to situated social conditions. And this remains a much-needed scholarly area for future research and theory building.

The analysis in this book further deepens the scope and conceptualization of accountability. West and Zimmerman (2009, 114) based their understanding of accountability on *congruency* between sex category and gender behavior, whereby the latter is orchestrated to be compatible with, and thus mutually constitute, the former. For West and Zimmerman (116), the key to conceptualizing "doing gender" is accountability to one's sex category membership or to the sex categories to which we are interactionally assigned.

Yet Jessie's and Morgan's life stories suggest that across social situations and contexts—from home to university—they were primarily accountable to *incongruency* between sex category and gender behavior. This raises the necessity of exploring when sex is judged to be congruent or incongruent with gender by copresent interactants, and future research on this aspect of sex and gender will also be extremely instructive.

Jessie and Morgan provide numerous examples of congruency/incongruency in accountability, such as in high school when Morgan adopted a "preppy-girl" feminine identity and practiced heteronormative congruency among sex, gender, and sexual identities. Much differently, in the setting of the LGBTQ+ and transmasculine groups, members were held accountable to diverse forms of sex/gender/sexual incongruency and fluidity, depending upon the specific group context. Nevertheless, in certain institutional contexts—such as the setting of Jessie's elementary and junior high schools—incongruency was policed and devalued by dominant boys/girls and was labeled *unaccountable* because her/his masculinity was not performed in and through a socially perceived male body. Alongside this, however, Jessie's tomboy identity was *accountable* within the context of her/his tomboy collective. In nonsexual social situations when Morgan described zirself as a "stealth dude," there existed congruence between sex and gender, and ze easily "passed" as an *accountable* male. Yet, in sexual social situations with certain straight women, incongruence between sex and gender occurred, leading Morgan to consider zir maleness as *unaccountable* (see further Schilt and Windsor 2014; Westbrook and Schilt 2014). What these examples indicate is that *both* congruence and incongruence between sex category and gender behavior can be essential—depending upon the context—for constructing accountability as well as unaccountability, and future research on such dynamics is needed.

The understanding of accountability is further advanced in this book by connecting it specifically with three identity formations. The notion of an *accountable identity* centers on sex, gender, and sexual identities—rather than simply gender—that are routinely acceptable to oneself and/or others within and/or across particular contexts. What we observe in the two life stories is Jessie and Morgan variably involved in a kaleidoscope of accountable identities, mainly because particular accountable identities become *unaccountable* when social interaction and/or the social context—and thus social structures—change. Although initially *all* the differing identities constructed by Jessie and Morgan over time and space were reflexively and routinely regarded as acceptable and thus routinely stabilized (for differing time frames), eventually each became unaccountable (except for their genderqueer identities), and a new identity was pursued. And this emphasis on both accountability and unaccountability, and when and why they specifically occur, is in need of further investigation and research.

Moreover, not all identity formations were based on accountability to a specific group, as some were unaccountable or accountable to oneself. For example, both Jessie and Morgan reflexively decided to practice hetero-sexuality and thus accountability, but eventually each rejected that form of sexuality, they became unaccountable to the heterosexual structure, and alternatively they were accountable to themselves. When Jessie read her/his body as unaccountably "girl" because of what she/he perceived as limited breast development—her/his tomboy friends never raised any issue about her/his body—eventually she/he judged him/herself accountable as a "girl who doesn't have breasts." The fact that Jessie did not possess a penis became the emblematic social sign for routinely retaining her/his mutually constituted accountable tomboy identity. And within the setting of the transmasculine university group, Jessie's masculine lesbian identity was designated unac-countable to her/him as Jessie now identified as a "both" genderqueer and thus was accountable to her/himself as well as members of the group. As a participant in zir LGBT group in high school, Morgan similarly reflexively decided that zir preppy-girl feminine identity was unaccountable to zem and instead reflexively decided to embody a "male" identity. While at university, Morgan determined zir "male" identity was unaccountable to zirself and instead constructed a genderqueer identity that was accountable to both zir-self and zir transmasculine friends. What these examples suggest is the need for more research on the relationship between accountability and identity formations and how individuals become unaccountable and accountable *to themselves*.

The new approach developed in this book additionally diverges from the "doing gender" perspective in a number of ways by building on scholarship addressing the significance of the body to sex, gender, and sexual practices and identities (e.g., Connell 1987, 1995; Lucal 1999; Budgeon 2003; Lorber and Moore 2011; Schilt 2010; Dozier 2005; Darwin 2017; shuster 2017; Meadow 2018; Risman 2018a). First, Jessie's and Morgan's bodies were implicated in more than doing gender; they were embroiled in *negating* gender—or what Barbee and Schrock (2019) label *ungendering*—and their bodies had implications far beyond gender, as their bodies were participants in sex, gender, and sexual identity formations. For example, as tomboys, Jessie and Morgan reflexively and routinely embodied a sex category of "girl," yet they simultaneously attempted to nullify embodiments of feminin-ity (in the home setting, Jessie adorned herself with feminine display). In early schooling, both reflexively did not want to look or act like a girl, and their routine bodily display of boyish clothing as well as routine masculine bodily practices were constructed in part to erase intimations of femininity.

And these data are similar to Pascoe's (2007) analysis of high school girls in a gay/straight alliance group. Rather than redefining embodied girlhood as "tough and powerful," Jessie's and Morgan's friends' enactments of an embodied tomboy identity served to denigrate femininity (2007, 117). Yet, eventually both Jessie and Morgan came to embody femininity (albeit in different capacities and from differing perspectives and understandings) as part of a future gender identity.

Second, the body is central to Jessie's and Morgan's changing sex, gender, and sexual identity constructions. For example, the sexed, gendered, and sexualized meanings of certain bodily parts and developments—such as breasts, menstruation, and penis—suggest a degree of bodily anxiety in the construction of sex, gender, and sexual identities because these body parts and functions are expected to be congruent with sexed and gendered enactments (Dozier 2005; Lorber and Moore 2011). What this signals is that the body, its changes, and its various parts are not neutral in constructing sex, gender, and sexual identities. Rather, bodies are agents of social practice that affect both reflexive and routine social action (Connell 1995), and such embodied changes are supported by scholarship on the gendered experiences of puberty (e.g., K. Martin 2018; Mora 2012). Bodies and their visible parts are agentic; they are participants in our recurring reflexive and routine self-attributions and impact identity formations. For example, sometimes bodies and their parts betray identities—such as when Jessie reflexively questioned whether or not she/he was a girl because of relatively small breasts, and when Morgan reflexively deliberated whether or not ze actually was a "man" because ze did not possess a "real penis" (see further Schilt and Windsor 2014).

Yet, the body and its parts do not simply restrict the construction of identities. It also occasionally proposes new configurations of identity. For example, Jessie described her/his relatively embodied small breasts as motivating reflexivity and the adoption of a new sexed identity as "a girl with small breasts," and Jessie's experiences with her/his female sexed body reflexively in part inspired her/his construction of a genderqueer identity. Morgan's changed female sexed body during puberty encouraged zir to reflexively embrace a preppy-girl feminine identity and in turn that same sexed body eventually resulted in reflexive feelings of "bodily incompleteness" and thus activated a transition to a male body.

Third, within the context of a genderqueer identity, Jessie routinely constructed a fluid body, discretely changing sexed, gendered, and sexualized identities through divergent bodily displays, manipulations, and meanings, while Morgan routinely embodied *at once* a variety of sexes, genders, and sexualities.

Fourth, Jessie and Morgan reflexively/routinely used or refused specific pronouns to help legitimate particular sexed bodies. When identifying as a tomboy and a masculine lesbian, Jessie utilized she/her/hers to signify "I'm a girl"; when publicly in drag Jessie refused any pronoun that undermined her/his political motives; and when involved in skoliosexuality, Jessie adopted specific binary feminine/masculine pronouns supporting particular gendered embodied sexual practices. Like Jessie, when identifying as a tomboy and as a feminine preppy girl Morgan adopted she/her/hers pronouns to represent zirself as a girl. After Morgan transitioned and embodied a "stealth dude" identity, ze utilized masculine pronouns of he/him/his. And following the adoption of a genderqueer identity, Morgan used ze, zem, and zir. Meadow (2018) documents similar alternating uses of gendered pronouns among young transgender people. Meadow (2018, 25) writes about one gender non-conforming young person: "Ari, age twelve, attended school as a boy, though his manner of dress and style of behavior remained markedly feminine. He vacillated between using male and female names and pronouns." Meadow scrupulously uses pronouns that reflect the identities and experiences of the young people in that study and acknowledges that in-use language makes this a difficult task.

Fifth, it is emphasized throughout the life stories that reflexivity and routine are part of the mind/body seamless whole, all inseparably linked, whereby mind and body live at once in the reflexive/routine social construction of sex, gender, and sexual embodied identities.

Sixth, to be "read" by copresent interactants as representing accountable identities, Jessie and Morgan both reflexively and routinely maintained situationally appropriate embodied displays and behaviors because the body is social, and social contexts are created through intercorporeality. Their sex, gender, and sexual identities were accomplished together—albeit variably—through the same embodied practices; they were mutually constituted, and their joint configuration materialized particular embodied identities.

Finally, as is evident in both Jessie's and Morgan's life histories, the body is agentic, a participant in the adoption of distinct genderqueer identity formations. For example, during social interaction in the university transmasculine group, Jessie reflexively and routinely "experimented" bodily by transitioning from female to male through binding and packing but eventually and reflexively decided against congruency and chose fluidity through the adoption of an embodied and routinely "both" genderqueer identity. When engaged in sexuality with male-bodied people, Jessie reflexively embodied masculinity by centering the gendered issue of being "in control" during the sexual encounter. In other words, the body impacted reflexivity/routine and conversely reflexivity/routine impacted the body. For Morgan, during sexuality with the "gay guy," their bodily sex was erased as the sexual interaction emphasized gender: "I was a girl and he was a boy, but we ignored that and just noticed our genders." Eventually, Morgan reflexively decided to transition and embody a male identity. Through top surgery and hormones Morgan's visible body "looked more masculine," and ze learned from zir "transguy" friends' new bodily skills so as to embody together sex (male) and gender (masculinity) identities as mutually constituted within the same practices. However, Morgan also described feeling not fully accountable as male and masculine during sexuality with certain straight women, and reflexively identified as a "neither" genderqueer.

The distinction between Jessie's notion of genderqueer as comprising *both* masculine and feminine identities alongside Morgan's conception as constituting *neither* masculine nor feminine identities offers a powerful illustration of Sedgwick's (1995) argument that masculinity and femininity are best understood orthogonally, rather than along a continuum. As Sedgwick writes,

> [I]nstead of being at opposite poles of the same axis, [masculinity and femininity] are actually in different, perpendicular dimensions, and therefore are independently variable. . . . One implication of [this] . . . is that not only are some people more masculine or more feminine than others, but some people are just more *gender-y* than others—whether the gender they manifest be masculine, feminine, both, or "and then some." (1995, 15–16)

Distinguishing between the different ways Jessie and Morgan make sense of their own genderqueer identities as *both* feminine and masculine (Jessie) or *neither* feminine nor masculine (Morgan) supports Sedgwick's argument about the orthogonality of masculinity and femininity. Additionally, it suggests great diversity within genderqueer identity formations, something future research will no doubt address in much more detail.

The above seven examples offer a collection of illustrations of how the body is essential to the construction and actuation of sex, gender, and sexual identities. Needless to say, there exists an absolute necessity for further research on how the body signifies sex, gender, and sexual identities, and how the body is agentic and thus a participant in differing ways during the social process of identity formation.

In "The Past," we concentrated on feminist *sociological* theories that examined gender in relation to reflexive and routine practices; however, feminists in other disciplines also theorized gender. The foremost among them is the philosopher Judith Butler (1990, 1993a). Butler is well known for her theory of gender performativity, which argues that through routine gender practices people create gender, and without such practices gender would not exist. For Butler, gender is constructed through performativity, gender produces the very thing it describes, and gender is fashioned by individuals engaging in gender practice. Similar to West and Zimmerman, Butler's position is that gender is not something an actor *is* but, rather, something an actor *does*.

Butler (1990, 25) specifically differs from West and Zimmerman, however, by arguing that "gender proves to be performative—that is, constituting the identity it is purported to be. In this sense, gender is always a doing, *though not a doing by a subject who might be said to preexist the deed*" (emphasis added). While we agree that gender identities (and sex and sexual identities) involve a routine "doing," for Butler there is no reflexivity prior to the doing of gender as individuals essentially are "cultural dopes" (Garfinkel 1967), empty vessels into which discourse pours gender (and sex and sexual) ideas, and they experience what Althusser (1970) labels "interpellation," in which bodies *unconsciously* act out those gender ideas. The process involves "a reiterative or citational practice by which discourse produces the effects that it names" (Butler 1993a, 2).

Jessie's and Morgan's life stories challenge Butler's perspective as they provide myriad examples of a *conscious* "doer behind the deed." For example, both Jessie and Morgan reflexively adopted at home a tomboy identity, they reflexively continued to practice that identity during early schooling, and they reflexively embraced heterosexuality. The life stories also provide evidence of reflexively questioning one's current identity; for example, when Jessie determined she/he lacked appropriate changes to her/his body during puberty, she/he reflexively doubted her/his identity as an accountable "girl," and after much internal deliberation, she/he changed that identity to "a different type of girl." Morgan experienced changes to zir body during early puberty that differed from what Jessie faced. Morgan reflexively read zir bodily changes as creating a more conventionally sexed female body, and thus ze reflexively adopted a preppy-girl feminine identity. In high school we also see reflexivity leading to two different identities for Jessie and Morgan: Jessie reflexively assumes a masculine lesbian identity while Morgan reflexively decides to transition to male and settles on constructing a stealth heteromasculine identity. Finally, at university Jessie reflexively rejects exclusive maleness and assumes a fluid "both" genderqueer identity, while Morgan reflexively abandons zir stealth heteromasculine identity and reflexively adopts a "neither" genderqueer identity. These examples demonstrate that both Jessie and Morgan reflexively negotiated different relational and discursive structures in a variety of contexts and, in the process, became the reflexive "doer" behind the routine "deed" of changing unaccountable, or maintaining accountable, sexed, gendered, and sexual identities. Many of these incidents also support shuster's (2017) notion of "self-enforcement accountability" whereby Jessie and Morgan hold themselves accountable through reflexively anticipating developing interactions. It would therefore be especially valuable to have more research on how individuals mobilize their sex, gender, and sexual identities as reflexive agents.

Butler (1990, xv) additionally argues that gender is performative in the sense that it is "manufactured through a sustained set of acts, posited through the gendered stylization of the body." And that performativity "consists of a reiteration of norms which precede, constrain, and exceed the performer and in that sense cannot be taken as the fabrication of the performer's 'will' or choice" (Butler 1993a, 234). Although Jessie and Morgan clearly "stylized" their bodies in ways that reflected and reproduced the variety of situational relational and discursive structures they encountered, such social action was not simply a "reiteration of norms" (i.e., *routine*) but, rather, was constructed through intertwining routine *and* reflexive practices. Jessie and Morgan constructed unreflexive conscious—not unconscious—sex, gender, and sexual routines that involved disciplined bodies actively performing accountable identities over time and space. The life stories identify diverse social signs that became contextual prompts and signals for fostering or reflexively editing and transforming specific gendered routines. Indeed, Jessie's and Morgan's life stories present numerous examples of each being confronted by several discursive structures simultaneously, and both Jessie and Morgan reflexively deciding which to identify with and which to reject. For example, in early schooling both Jessie and Morgan reflexively rejected the popular "preppy-girl" feminine identity discourse and instead maintained tomboy identities. And later in junior high and high school, when faced with heterosexual discursive structures, Jessie and Morgan reflexively adopted this discourse but quickly rejected and separated themselves from this discursive structure. It is therefore vitally important that researchers further investigate how, why, and when individuals reflexively adopt and abandon particular discursive and relational structures; how accountability constrains, enables, and stabilizes unreflexive routine; and how reflexive and routine practices are symbiotically interconnected and coconstitutive within various identity formations.

Finally, Butler (1990) argues that individuals should destabilize the sex, gender, and sexual hegemonic binaries by making

> *gender trouble*, not through the strategies that figure a utopian beyond, but through the mobilization, subversive confusion, and proliferation of precisely those constitutive categories that seek to keep gender in its place by posturing as the foundational illusions of identity. (1990, 33–34)

Butler reasons that asserting subversive sex, gender, and sexual practices will undermine any notion that hegemonic binaries re "natural." To adopt a subversive sex, gender, and/or sexuality, however, one must first reflexively consider the troublemaking social action.[1] Recall Jessie's discussion about when she/he and genderqueer friends routinely went out at night in drag in multiple ways. Jessie stated that it was through reflexivity that they decided to do drag in various styles so as to "disrupt the normal. It's all about making people question me and themselves." Jessie and his/her friends reflexively alternated among masculine, feminine, and androgynous performances, pronouns, and identities consistent with the particular context, and while these shifts occurred routinely, Jessie described them as accompanied by reflexive intention—"troubling" sex, gender, and sexuality as both routine *and* reflexive. Thus, an important area for future research would be to examine exactly when, why, and how individuals decide to participate in such subversive sex, gender, and sexual practices. When, in other words, do individuals elect to trouble sex, gender, and sexuality, and what role do both reflexivity and routine play in this dynamic process?

The two life histories also demonstrate that the *salience* of sex, gender, and sexuality identities is important contextually because each is shifting, yet ubiquitous—that is, the significance of each is fluid and shifts from context to context. For example, in one situation sex and gender identities (but not sexuality identities) may mutually constitute one another; in another, gender and sexuality identities (but not sex identities) may mutually constitute each other; and at other times, all three identities may mutually constitute each other. In other words, sex, gender, and sexuality identities are not absolutes and are not always equally significant in every social setting in which individuals participate—they *mutually constitute* each other in differing ways depending upon the social situation.[2] And Jessie's and Morgan's life histories demonstrate this variable mutual constitution of sex, gender, and sexuality. For example, both Jessie and Morgan at home and during elementary and junior high school accomplished together sex (girl) and gender (masculinity) identities through the same practices, mutually constituting a fully embodied tomboy identity. That is, the mutual constitution of two identities in the same practices enabled or made possible the actuation of a new and particularized identity. In high school, however, Jessie accomplished together sex (girl), gender (masculinity), and sexuality (homosexuality) identities in the same practices, and the joint configuration materialized into an accountable and embodied masculine lesbian identity. When Morgan was in high school, ze accomplished together sex (girl), gender (femininity), and sexuality (heterosexuality) identities in the same practices so as to mutually constitute an accountable and embodied preppy-girl feminine identity, yet in due course, ze nullified sex and fashioned the mutual constitution of gender (masculinity) and sexuality (skoliosexual) identities when engaging in embodied sexuality with the "gay guy." Eventually, Morgan accomplished together sex (male), gender (masculinity), and sexuality (heterosexuality) identities through the same practices so as to mutually constitute an accountable and embodied heteromasculine "stealth dude" identity. Finally, within the setting of the university, Jessie accomplished together the fluidity of sex, gender, and sexual identities so as to mutually constitute an accountable and embodied *both* genderqueer identity, while Morgan accomplished together a combination of sexes, genders, and sexual identities in the same practices that mutually constituted an accountable and embodied *neither* genderqueer identity. This demonstrates the need for further research into the variable mutual constitution of sex, gender, and sexual identities.

The life-history data of Jessie and Morgan additionally allow us to consider the different—and often hierarchical—in-school relations among girls and femininities they each discussed. For example, in elementary and junior high school Jessie and her/his friends experienced bullying for constructing a tomboy identity and thus were subordinated by the popular dominant girls (and boys) as lesser girls. The tomboys and dominant girls represented two different types that were differentiated through their gender constructions—masculinity and femininity, respectively. Jessie and her/his tomboy friends faced bullying exacted for failure to conform to dominant and accountable sex/gender displays and behaviors and for practicing masculinity in and through a female body, and the bullying contributed to maintaining and sustaining unequal structured relations among girls within these settings. The popular feminine girls set the standards for dominant and thus accountable display and behavior in school. Social hierarchies developed in relation to embodied sex/gender identities, and such bodily differentiation affirmed inequality among/between girls. It therefore would be beneficial to have further research on the inequalities among girls in elementary and secondary schools, especially regarding relations among dominant and subordinate identities.

The data from the interviews further suggested that dominant feminine girls in these settings are not solely established through bodily displays and behavior but also through distancing oneself from subordinate forms of girl embodiment.[3] And one way to accomplish such distancing is by bullying tomboys, a practice that situates dominant girl/feminine embodiment as "superior" to "inferior" subordinated girl/masculine displays/behaviors. Here we see an example of masculinity—when practiced in and through a female body—that actually is subordinated to femininity when also practiced in and through girls' bodies. Bullying, then, is a form of power whereby dominant girls command and control interaction among girls, exercising a localized dominant position by policing the intercorporeal boundaries of accountable sex/gender display and practice and simultaneously demarcating subordinate delegitimated tomboys. For Jessie, sex and gender accountability at school were based on an understanding of sex/gender relations emphasizing strict adherence to hegemonic binaries (see further Pascoe 2007, 2013; Klein 2013; Budgeon 2014; Ispa-Landa and Oliver 2020). And consistent with other work on the social subordination of certain girls at school (Thorne 1993; Bettie

2002; Pascoe 2007; Garcia 2012; Messerschmidt 2012), Jessie's tomboy collective was subordinated in the in-school clique social structure.

The dominant girls then represented the most *celebrated* form of femininity in these settings, yet they did not *in and of themselves* or in relation to same-sex classmates legitimate gender inequality between boys and girls. Such legitimacy would only occur if these dominant girls were positioned in a subordinate status to dominant boys, and if so, that relationship would construct hegemonic masculinity and emphasized femininity (not *hegemonic* femininity), or unequal gender relations between boys and girls. This conceptualization is consistent with Connell's (1987, 187) position that "there is no femininity that holds among women the position held by hegemonic masculinity among men." This is so because relations among and between femininities do *not* legitimate unequal gender relations between men and women, masculinity and femininity. Although the concept of hegemonic masculinity was originally formulated by Connell in tandem with the concept of hegemonic femininity, it was soon renamed "emphasized" femininity to acknowledge and underline unequal gender relations between men and women, between masculinity and femininity, and among masculinities (Connell and Messerschmidt 2005). Scholars who use "hegemonic femininity" then often miss the significance of the concept of "hegemonic" for signifying the *legitimation* of unequal relations between men and women, between masculinity and femininity, and among masculinities (see also Messerschmidt 2018a).

In addition, concentrating on so-called hegemonic femininity misses the relations between two dominant girls simultaneously, such as what Morgan experienced. In Morgan's early schooling, ze likewise participated in a tomboy group, yet ze was not bullied like Jessie and her/his tomboy friends. Indeed, Morgan's tomboy group was considered one of two dominant groups—primarily because they were the top athletes in the school—yet that group still stood in unequal relation to the preppy-girl feminine dominant group. Morgan identifies a status difference between the heteronormative preppies and the tomboy collective. The latter girls, then, in a different way than Jessie's tomboy collective, were constructed as lesser girls. This is consistent with Pascoe's (2007) study of a US high school, whereby girls' enactments of masculinity were afforded very different kinds of status based on where they fell in the school's clique structure: the basketball girls' enactments of masculinity (similar to Morgan's tomboy gender practice) were accountable while enactments of masculinity by girls in the school's gay/straight alliance (similar to Jessie's tomboy gender practice) were not. Morgan's tomboy collective was accountable because of their athletic distinction, yet in relation to the preppy-feminine girls their status as girls was aberrant. Clearly, then, more research is needed with regard to when girls' constructions of masculinities in school—as well as outside school—are accountable and when they are not, and even when accountable they may not be fully acceptable.

In addition to the above, recent gender research on the practices of girls and women has carefully examined the historical interplay of emphasized femininities and hegemonic masculinities. For example, Carlson (2010) demonstrated how women involved in roller derby reflexively interrogate a localized emphasized femininity without undermining the hegemonic masculine/emphasized feminine unequal gender binary; Currier (2013) examined the college hookup culture and showed how it authorizes men to reflexively and routinely construct a localized hegemonic masculinity and women reflexively and routinely orchestrate a localized emphasized femininity; and Hamilton (2020) revealed that heterosexual women practicing professional mixed martial arts construct a localized masculinity, yet when they are outside the athletic arena in their intimate partner relations, these same women reflexively and routinely fashion a localized emphasized femininity in subordination to localized hegemonically masculine men.[4]

Not surprising, Jessie and Morgan briefly practiced emphasized femininity, both within the context of heterosexuality. In junior high school, Jessie reflexively attempted to attach heteronormative practices to her/his routine tomboy identity and eventually met and dated several boys. The boys pressured Jessie to look more feminine, and they subordinated Jessie's opinions and "decided everything"—where they would go, what they would do, and when they would kiss and have sex. The boys Jessie dated then attempted to construct a dominating hegemonically masculine and emphasized feminine relationship with her/him through the practice of heterosexuality, and Jessie for a short time jointly constructed that unequal relationship: in relation to these boys, Jessie fashioned emphasized femininity. This particular form of hegemonic masculinity was "dominating" because the boys were commanding and controlling the specific sexual interaction, they exercised power and control over Jessie and the social situation, and they called the shots and ran the show. Yet Jessie reflexively worked out that she/he wanted to equally decide what she/he would and would not do together and she/he wanted to be sexually assertive. But the boys disallowed such agency, so Jessie broke up with each of them and completely disassociated her/himself from the structured heteronormative hegemonic gender and sexual binaries.

In high school, Morgan routinely practiced a preppy-girl heterofemininity. Although ze found the relationship with the boys ze dated close and friendly, ze never enjoyed engaging in heterosexuality with them. Morgan felt that ze was not "being seen," and the sexual interaction did not "fit" because the boys feminized zir as an object, disallowing zir to decide how ze wanted to be touched and interacted with sexually. The sexual interaction with the high school boys involved Morgan being expected to routinely participate in a dominating hegemonically masculine and emphasized feminine relationship through heterosexuality. Yet, after a short time, Morgan—like Jessie—reflexively determined that doing so limited zir sexual agency, and therefore, ze reflexively decided to end each relationship and likewise completely disassociated zirself from the structured heteronormative hegemonic gender and sexual binaries. As such, we need much more research on how reflexive and routine practices are related to the social construction of dominant and emphasized femininities, as well as when actors separate and detach themselves from particular social structures.

In a series of papers, Rhea Asley Hoskin (2017, 2019, 2020) examined the practice of "femmephobia," or the devaluation and regulation of femininity, and documents masculine privilege across LGBTQ+ communities. Hoskin found that both gay men, lesbians, and transgender people commonly consider masculinity to be much more attractive than femininity, and they place more value on masculinity than on femininity. Hoskin also shows that this privileging of masculinity often generates feelings of unaccountability among, and impacts the mental self-being of, femme-identified individuals. Hoskin details, for example, that many femme-identified individuals enter into relationships with butch-identified individuals, yet confirms that femme is a "form of queer femininity that cannot be pinned down to a singular embodiment or relationship" (2020, 2321). Despite this variability in femme identities, Hoskin (2335) further shows that within LGBTQ+ communities, for every measure of masculine privilege, there is an equivalent measure of feminine subordination, and this gender binary functions to help maintain gender and sexual hegemony (see further, Hoskin and Blair 2021). In relation to Hoskin's work, what the two life stories reveal is that within every institution and thus gender regime Jessie and Morgan participated—from family through different forms of schooling and including the LGBT and transmasculine groups—they encountered both relational and discursive structures that privileged masculinity by placing more value on masculinity than on femininity. And this relational and discursive structural ascendancy and thus importance of masculinity was embodied in the vast majority of Jessie's and Morgan's identities, and it is through those identities that the various relational and discursive structures were constituted. Clearly, then, we need further research on the subordination of femme and femininity and, thus, the primacy of masculinity both within and without LGBTQ+ communities.

The life story of Jessie adds to Hoskin's work in another important way. Not only did Jessie participate (albeit briefly) in her/his subordination to masculine privilege through heterosexuality, recall that Jessie reported reflexively identifying as a "masculine lesbian" in high school, detailing her/his involvement in a binary same-sex relationship in which the partners were "read" by copresent interactants as a "normal" masculine/feminine couple with female bodies. Same-sex sexual relationships were accountable in Jessie's high school within a heteronormative framework in which one member is "masculine" and the other "feminine." In this sense, Jessie's partnership with her/his girlfriend satisfied structured heteronormative criteria, and consequently Jessie and her/his girlfriend fashioned localized "masculine lesbian" and "femme lesbian" identities, respectively.

Jessie's relationship with her/his girlfriend reiterated a form of gender hegemony. Jessie reflexively and routinely saw her/himself as the assertive partner who derives masculine hegemonic power through the dependent/subordinate status of her/his emphasized feminine girlfriend; Jessie's girlfriend reflexively and routinely respects, honors, and yields to her/his caring guidance, protection, and support. The relationship therefore replicates gendered forms of hegemony and subordination that perpetuate hierarchy and inequality, even when motivated by benevolent protectionist impulses (Messerschmidt 2018a). Femme subordination, masculine hegemony, and heteronormativity thus proceed from the position of compassionate protector. The relationship Jessie described centers on routinely defined and enacted "inferior" feminine and "superior" masculine practices, a relationship that constructs a distinct form of localized emphasized femininity in relation to Jessie's protectionist hegemonic masculinity. And what this case further suggests is that girls and women are never in the position to be "hegemonic" unless they construct "superior" masculine qualities in relation to "inferior" feminine qualities.

Abundant research is necessary by gender scholars on hegemonic masculinities and how certain unequal and hierarchical gender relations become legitimated at local levels. It would be extremely helpful to have, for example, additional research on when and how girls and women construct hegemonic masculinity. And included here are of course research endeavors that examine the differences among hegemonic masculinities. For example, Jessie's and Morgan's life stories distinguish between "dominating" and "protective" forms of hegemonic masculinities and accordingly differing types of gendered power. The heterosexual boys who engaged in "sexuality" with Jessie and Morgan consolidated their hegemonic power through *dominating* all aspects of the sexual interactions; in contrast, the distinct type of hegemonic power found during Jessie's sexual interaction with her/his girlfriend was established through benevolent *protection*, which emphasized caring, guidance, and support. This form of hegemonic masculinity challenges notions of hegemonic masculinity as exclusively pernicious and noxious.

The life histories of Jessie and Morgan establish how sex, gender, and sexual identities are products of both reflexive and routine social actions, and are situationally shaped, subject to interactional accountability, and both constrained and enabled by contextual relational and discursive social structures. Although each of Jessie's and Morgan's differing identities were contextually configured, the specific social situations they encountered—from family life through high school—*were structured exclusively by male/ female, masculine/feminine, and heterosexual/homosexual hegemonic binaries*. During much of their lives, then, Jessie and Morgan reflexively drew exclusively from hegemonic binaries embedded in relational and discursive social structures to assemble and shape their various sex, gender, and sexual identities. For example, both Jessie and Morgan reflexively and routinely fashioned tomboy identities within the family and into elementary school that mutually constituted a redesigned configuration of binary sex (girl) and gender (masculine) identities. In high school, Jessie initially reflexively and routinely affixed heterosexuality to her/his tomboy identity, but quickly rejected heterosexuality and reflexively adopted homosexuality and routinely practiced a reworked binary-informed "masculine lesbian" identity. In junior high school, Morgan eventually reflexively rejected zir tomboy identity and embraced routinely a "preppy-girl feminine" identity that mutually constituted the heteronormative binary categories of sex (girl), gender (feminine), and sexuality (heterosexuality). In high school, however, Morgan reflexively switched zir identity by commencing a transition to the opposite sex and routinely and mutually constituted the heteronormative binary categories of sex (male), gender (masculine), and sexuality (heterosexuality). What these examples demonstrate is that from the family through high school, Jessie and Morgan constructed different arrangements of sex, gender, and sexual hegemonic binary identities—both congruent and incongruent—because the contextual interactions, accountability demands, and relational and discursive social structures defined possible identity formations exclusively in terms of these binary categories. Moreover, it was easy for their identities to be "read" or "determined" (Westbrook and Schilt 2014) as intended because copresent interactants had the binary knowledge to recognize properly and intelligibly each component of the mutual constitution of sex, gender, and sexuality. It therefore would be valuable if further research specifically examined how individuals refashion hegemonic sex, gender, and sexual binaries into new configured identities, and whether or not interactants within the same social setting correctly "read" those identities as planned.

While attending university, however, the social context dramatically changed to a separatist milieu that emphasized a variety of hegemonic binary and nonhegemonic nonbinary identities. Jessie and Morgan joined university groups that emphasized trans-affirmative styles of interaction, accountability demands, and relational and discursive social structures. For example, the new knowledge about alternative sex, gender, and sexual identities led Jessie to "try on" binary congruency between sex (male) and gender (masculine) to see if she/he wanted to fully transition. But after numerous such "experiments," Jessie reflexively decided not to transition and instead identified as genderqueer—which, for Jessie, entailed identifying with *both* femininity and masculinity. Morgan became a member of zir high school LGBT group and eventually decided to transition to "male" by having chest surgery, taking hormones, and adopting masculine pronouns. At university Morgan practiced a "stealth masculinity" and joined a transmasculine group whereby ze learned how to "pass" in *nonsexual* social situations, yet because ze did not possess a "real penis," ze felt zir binary heteromasculine maleness was challenged in *sexual* social situations. Moreover, some "transguys" questioned Morgan about zir past, and ze reflexively concluded from such interaction that ze was required to selectively narrate an exclusive male past and to erase all the former "female and feminine stuff." These transguys, then, were attempting to hold Morgan accountable to a "trans narrative" by requiring zem to recount a history exhibiting no interest, at any time, in anything female and/or feminine. This is an example of what shuster (2017) refers to as "other-enforcement accountability" whereby Morgan is being held accountable to hegemonic binary congruence. Through internal conversations, however, Morgan reflexively resisted that narrative and attempt at regulating zir identity formation—ze determined ze was not "trans enough" (Garrison 2018)—and instead identified as genderqueer. To Morgan, genderqueer identity entailed identifying explicitly with *neither* femininity *nor* masculinity. It would therefore be helpful if future scholars would examine closely the ongoing interactions in trans communities and determine if similar regulatory processes continue and, if so, how they impact the reflexive and routine practices of community members.

It was within the setting of LGBT and transmasculine groups that Jessie and Morgan reflexively and routinely practiced genderqueer. Through interaction within these groups, Jessie and Morgan understood that they could be whatever they wanted to be, that they could create their own embodied narrative. Consequently, both designed distinct genderqueer configurations of identity that were primarily accountable to themselves, and those identity formations mutually constituted a variety of different identities. For Jessie, being a "both" genderqueer involved the fluctuating mutual constitution of binary and nonbinary sex (male and female), gender (masculine, feminine, and androgyny), and sexual (skoliosexual/polyamory/pansexuality) identities. For Morgan, being a "neither" genderqueer entailed the mutual constitution of particular nonbinary sex (androgynous), gender (maxigender), and sexual (skoliosexual/pansexual) identities. In other words, Jessie and Morgan reflexively decided which identities were to be included in their all-embracing genderqueer identities, and that particular reflexive process is significantly different from their selection of all identities practiced prior to university. It would therefore be helpful if future research examined when and why people simply reflexively adopt the available possible identities in certain contexts and when and why they reflexively construct individually assembled identities in other contexts.

Throughout their lives, Jessie's and Morgan's sex, gender, and sexual identities were not determined and tenacious since birth, but rather their kaleidoscopic identities were embedded in changing social contexts involving endlessly becoming, consistently formulating new identities. At each major juncture in their lives, the specific social contexts offered Jessie and Morgan places within the sex, gender, and sexual hierarchies, but Jessie and Morgan reflexively determined how to respond to those offers in significantly different ways and, thus, to routinely practice particular identities. Indeed, within each new gender regime, their identities were in the midst of becoming something new, eventually morphing into fresh and new genderqueer identity formations. And the diverse identities of Jessie and Morgan were embodied through reflexive and routine practices as well as changing gender regimes.

Although Jessie and Morgan constructed accountable genderqueer identities *within* the LGBT and transmasculine groups in which they participated, they faced problems orchestrating a genderqueer identity when interacting in milieus *outside* such groups. For example, when Jessie ventured outside the transmasculine group to work at her/his part-time job, she/he reflexively interacted as an accountable woman. Anticipating the changing context—and thus practicing "self-enforcement accountability" (shuster 2017)—Jessie reflexively determined that an androgynous identity in the workplace setting would be unrecognizable and thus unaccountable, and therefore Jessie reflexively and routinely fashioned a well-defined female identity in that site. Jessie specifically fashioned an identity that would be intelligible to her/his coworkers so they could have no problem determining Jessie's mutually constituted sex and gender. Morgan emphasized in the interviews that outside the transmasculine group other people have a hard time "reading" zir as genderqueer because "I have so many bodies and so many past experiences all wrapped into one." In such "outside" settings, Morgan practices genderqueerness yet pointed to an example of unaccountability as a genderqueer customer in a gay bar. In this setting, ze is not recognized by other customers as genderqueer, but rather patrons tend to "misrecognize" (Pfeffer 2014) Morgan as, for example, an effeminate guy, a transman, a transwoman, or as butch.[5] To members of the transmasculine group, these varying identities were intelligible to them as part of Morgan's mutually constituted "neither" genderqueer identity. But for customers in the bar, Morgan's genderqueer identity is determined to be imperceptible and thus unseen. What this represents is that when individuals construct unrecognizable identities, copresent interactants often assign whatever identity reasonably seems "closest" (Garrison 2018). Accordingly, the customers at the bar are "determining gender" by placing Morgan in a gender identity that seems most intelligible and recognizable to them, a process replete with violence, injury, and accident (Westbrook and Schilt 2014). Indeed, both life stories demonstrate how accountability is unavoidable. This is an area in need of much research on these types of interactions, and how and why individuals recognize the intended identity, and if they do not, how and why they respond in particular ways.

Today, universities in the Global North have become prime social settings for the development and proliferation of new nonhegemonic nonbinary identity formations, and a diversity of these identities have increased rapidly. As Matthew Gutmann (2019) points out, university students born in the 1990s (as Jessie and Morgan were) are "pioneering" new ways of constructing sex, gender, and sexual identities. An increasing number of students are rejecting the hegemonic sex, gender, and sexual binaries, and thereby "challenging either-or restrictions and dichotomous ways of dividing up the world between two neat groups of men and women. . . . the demand to 'break down the binary!' is an urgent and righteous objective" by a growing number of university students (2019, 231).

In addition to university settings, young people have come to routinely practice nonbinary sexes, genders, and sexualities through social media, and Rob Cover's (2016, 2018, 2019) work has been prominent in documenting this development. What Cover examines is how the emergence of social media has enabled different voices to gather together for the purpose of collectively sharing alternative ideas about sex, gender, and sexuality. Such discursive interaction "involves opportunities not just for encountering and reading identity discourses," it additionally allows all involved to communicate "as co-creative participants" (2019, 65). Cover argues that the new nonbinary sex, gender, and sexual identities are in response to the reflexive perception that hegemonic binaries are inadequate—participants have found themselves unable to "fit" within these binaries, and therefore, the new identities are not simply "theatrics of taste, style, or nuance (e.g., sapiosexual aromantic demiboy) overlaid on a categorical real (e.g., unattached lesbian woman)" (2018, 281). Rather, and as observed with Jessie and Morgan, the new nonbinary identities involve the declaration that they finally found the "real me," there is a deeply felt attachment to these nonbinary identities, which are extremely "meaningful for a very large number of people" (281). The result has been an escalating reflexive acceptance, and a flourishing routine practice, of nonhegemonic nonbinary sex, gender, and sexual identities (as mentioned in "Theory and Method"). And, of course, we need much more life-history work on the relationship among the reflexive adoption, continuation, and routine practice of nonbinary sex, gender, and sexual identities.

Although university and social media milieus open up space for the disruption of hegemonic binaries, the male/female, masculine/feminine, and heterosexual/homosexual binaries continue to retain their hegemonic position in the sex, gender, and sexual hierarchies, and there exists no evidence that this is about to change. Indeed, because of the always possible unaccountability of nonbinary identities *outside* trans-affirmative social settings, there has been little challenge to the unequal relationship between hegemonic binary identities and nonhegemonic nonbinary identities (Lorber 2018, 2022; Risman, Myers, and Sin 2018). As Risman, Myers, and Sin (2018, 283) point out, rather than exploding hegemonic binary categories, choosing a nonhegemonic nonbinary identity "allows liberty for some without attacking stereotypes or constraints for most others." To be sure, neither Jessie nor Morgan—or others identifying as genderqueer (see Risman 2018b; Cover 2019)—seems interested in undoing, but rather increasing, the scope and diversity of sex, gender, and sexual identities. Today, young people at universities and as participants on social media are more attentive to reflexively and routinely practicing neoliberal *individualized* identities than they are working *collectively* to dismantle the hegemonic binaries. The emphasis is on personal choice as a way to construct a meaningful and habitable life. And such a reflexive individual decision is conceptualized as liberating, irrespective of their ongoing subordination to the hegemonic binaries.

To challenge sex, gender, and sexual hegemony, then, what this book points to is not simply exclusive support for the diversification of sex, gender, and sexual identities—although this is essential—but, rather, the promotion of *diversity with equality*—not only between binary identities but between binary and nonbinary identities as well as among nonbinary identities. We need to visualize a world of equality in which we also champion diversity. To paraphrase Judith Lorber (2022, 84), our goal at present must not be a world without diverse sexes, genders, and sexualities but, rather, must be a world without sex, gender, and sexual inequality.

NOTES

1. As with Garfinkel's (1967) analysis of Agnes's understanding of gender, individuals whose identities are cast as socially "subversive" might structurally be required to reflexively consider their sex/gender in ways similar to those who identify within hegemonic sex, gender, and sexual binaries. Even here, however, we would suggest that this is best understood as a potential difference in the *type* or *degree* of reflexivity rather than in its presence or absence.

2. Indeed, this supports Westbrook and Schilt's (2014) argument that institutional contexts play a crucial role in the process of what they refer to as "determining gender."

3. Among the new work examining inequality among and between femininities is Ispa-Landa and Oliver's (2020) research on hierarchies between femininities in their study of collegiate sororities in the United States. They provide new ideas that build on existing theorizations of femininities, gender relations, and inequality more generally.

4. For further work on emphasized femininity, see Domeneghetti 2017; Hechavarria and Ingram 2016; Kostas 2019; Messerschmidt 2010, 2012, 2014, 2016, 2018a, 2018b; Silva 2008; Talbot and Quayle 2010; Wolkomir 2012.

5. Pursuing identity formations that push against hegemonic sex/gender binary relations require kinds of reflexivity less structurally essential for other identity formations. Pfeffer's (2012) study of cisgender women in relationships with transgender men illustrates this dynamic well. Pfeffer considers the strategies these cisgender women deploy to make their identities and relationships intelligible in ways that similarly push against the hegemonic sex/gender/sexual binaries. Pfeffer describes twin strategies she refers to as "normative resistance" (whereby cisgender women resisted "social misrecognition as unremarkably heterosexual" [2012, 581]) and "inventive pragmatism" (whereby cisgender women described sometimes leaning on such misrecognition "to access regulated social institutions, resources, and technologies" [2012, 588]).

References

Acker, J. 1989. "The Problem with Patriarchy." *Sociology* 23 (2): 235–40.

Adkins, L. 2004. "Reflexivity: Freedom or Habit of Gender?" *Sociological Review* 52 (2): 191–210.

Agarwal, B. 1988. *Structures of Patriarchy.* New York: Cambridge University Press.

Althusser, L. 1970. *Lenin and Philosophy and Other Essays.* New York: Monthly Review Press.

Archer, M. 2000. *Being Human: The Problem of Agency.* Cambridge: Cambridge University Press.

———. 2003. *Structure, Agency, and the Internal Conversation.* New York: Cambridge University Press.

———. 2007. *Making Our Way through the World: Human Reflexivity and Human Mobility.* New York: Cambridge University Press.

———, ed. 2010. *Conversations about Reflexivity.* New York: Routledge.

———. 2012. *The Reflexive Imperative in Late Modernity.* New York: Cambridge University Press.

———. 2013. "Reflexivity." *Sociopedia.isa*, 1–14. https://doi.org/10.1177/205684601373.

Barbee, H., and D. Schrock. 2019. "Un/Gendering Social Selves: How Nonbinary People Navigate and Experience a Binarily Gendered World." *Sociological Forum* 34 (3): 572–93.

Beechy, V. 1987. *Unequal Work.* London: Verso.

Beirne, P., and J. W. Messerschmidt. 2015. *Criminology: A Sociological Approach.* New York: Oxford University Press.

Benston, M. 1969. "The Political Economy of Women's Liberation." *Monthly Review* 21 (4): 13–27.

Bettie, J. 2002. *Women without Class: Girls, Race, and Identity.* Berkeley: University of California Press.

Bourdieu, P. 1977. *Outline of a Theory of Practice.* Translated by R. Nice. New York: Cambridge University Press.

———. 1984. *Distinction.* Translated by R. Nice. New York: Routledge and Kegan Paul.

———. 1990. *In Other Words.* Translated by M. Adamson. Cambridge: Polity Press.

————. 1998. *Practical Reason.* Translated by R. Johnson et al. Cambridge: Polity Press.

————. (1997) 2000. *Pascalian Meditations.* Translated by R. Nice. Stanford, CA: Stanford University Press. Citations refer to the 2000 translation.

Bridges, T. 2009. "Gender Capital and Male Bodybuilders." *Body & Society* 15 (1): 83–107.

————. 2014. "A Very 'Gay' Straight? Hybrid Masculinities, Sexual Aesthetics, and the Changing Relationship between Masculinity and Homophobia." *Gender & Society* 28 (1): 58–82.

Bridges, T., and J. W. Messerschmidt. 2017. "Joan Acker and the Shift from Patriarchy to Gender." *Gender, Work & Organization* 26 (12): 1773–75.

Bridges, T., and C. J. Pascoe. 2018. "On the Elasticity of Gender Hegemony: Why Hybrid Masculinities Fail to Undermine Gender and Sexual Inequality." In *Gender Reckonings: New Social Theory and Research*, edited by J. W. Messerschmidt, P. Y. Martin, M. A. Messner, and R. Connell, 254–74. New York: New York University Press.

Brown, B. 1988. "Review of *Capitalism, Patriarchy, and Crime.*" *International Journal of the Sociology of Law* 16 (3): 408–12.

Brownmiller, S. 1975. *Against Our Will: Men, Women and Rape.* New York: Simon & Schuster.

Budgeon, S. 2003. "Identity as an Embodied Event." *Body & Society* 9 (1): 35–55.

————. 2014. "The Dynamics of Gender Hegemony." *Sociology* 48: 317–34.

————. 2015. "Theorizing Subjectivity and Feminine Embodiment: Feminist Approaches and Debates." In *Handbook of Children and Youth Studies*, edited by J. Wyn and H. Cahill. New York: Springer.

Burawoy, M. 2012. "The Roots of Domination: Beyond Bourdieu and Gramsci." *Sociology* 46 (2): 187–206.

Butler, J. 1990. *Gender Trouble.* New York: Routledge.

————. 1993a. *Bodies That Matter.* New York: Routledge.

————. 1993b. "Imitation and Gender Insubordination." In *The Lesbian and Gay Studies Reader*, edited by H. Abelove, M. A. Barale, and D. M. Halperin, 307–20. London: Routledge.

Carlson, J. 2010. "The Female Signifiant in All-Women's Amateur Roller Derby." *Sociology of Sport Journal* 27 (4): 428–40.

Caron, C. O. 2013. "Reflexivity at Work: Making Sense of Mannheim's, Garfinkel's, Gouldner's, and Bourdieu's Sociology." PhD diss., Carleton University, Ottawa, Canada.

Carrigan, T., R. Connell, and J. Lee. 1985. "Toward a New Sociology of Masculinity." *Theory and Society* 14 (5): 551–604.

————. 1987. "Hard and Heavy: Toward a New Sociology of Masculinity." In *Beyond Patriarchy*, edited by M. Kaufman. New York: Oxford University Press.

Cealey Harrison, W. 2006. "The Shadow and the Substance: The Sex/Gender Debate." In *Handbook of Gender and Women's Studies*, edited by K. Davis, M. Evans, and J. Lorber, 35–52. Thousand Oaks, CA: Sage.

Collins, P. H. 1990. *Black Feminist Thought: Knowledge, Consciousness, and the Politics of Empowerment*. London: HarperCollins Academic.

Connell, R. 1985a. "Theorizing Gender." *Sociology* 19 (2): 260–72.

———. 1985b. *Teachers' Work*. Sydney: Allen & Unwin.

———. 1987. *Gender and Power: Society, the Person, and Sexual Politics*. Sydney: Allen & Unwin.

———. 1995. *Masculinities*. Stanford, CA: Stanford University Press.

———. 1998. "Masculinities and Globalization." *Men and Masculinities* 1 (1): 3–23.

———. 2000. *The Men and the Boys*. Sydney: Allen & Unwin.

———. 2002. *Gender*. Cambridge: Polity Press.

———. 2004. "Encounters with Structure." *International Journal of Qualitative Studies in Education* 17 (1): 11–28.

———. 2007. "News from the Coalface: Experiences of Gender Reform by the Staff of Public Sector Agencies." *International Feminist Journal of Politics* 9 (2): 137–53.

———. 2012. "Transsexual Women and Feminist Thought: Toward New Understanding and New Politics." *Signs: Journal of Women in Culture and Society* 37 (4): 857–81.

———. 2014. *Gender*. 2nd ed. Cambridge: Polity Press.

———. 2021. *Gender*. 4th ed. Cambridge: Polity Press.

Connell, R., D. J. Ashenden, S. Kessler, and G. W. Dowsett. 1982. *Making the Difference: Schools, Families and Social Division*. Sydney: Allen & Unwin.

Connell, R., and J. W. Messerschmidt. 2005. "Hegemonic Masculinity: Rethinking the Concept." *Gender & Society* 19 (6): 829–59.

Cossins, A., and M. Plummer. 2018. "Masculinity and Sexual Abuse: Explaining the Transition from Victim to Offender." *Men and Masculinities* 21 (2): 163–88.

Cover, R. 2016. *Digital Identities: Creating and Communicating the Online Self*. New York: Elsevier.

———. 2018. "The Proliferation of Gender and Sexual Identities, Categories and Labels among Young People." In *Youth, Sexuality and Sexual Citizenship*, edited by P. Aggleton, R. Cover, D. Leahy, D. Marshall, and M. L. Rasmussen, 278–90. New York: Routledge.

———. 2019. *Emergent Identities: New Sexualities, Genders and Relationships in a Digital Era*. New York: Routledge.

Crenshaw, K. 1989. "Demarginalizing the Intersection of Race and Sex: A Black Feminist Critique of Antidiscrimination Doctrine, Feminist Theory, and Anti-racist Politics." *University of Chicago Legal Forum* 1989 (1): 139–67.

Crossley, N. 1995. "Body Techniques, Agency and Intercorporeality: On Goffman's *Relations in Public*." *Sociology* 29 (1): 133–49.

———. 2001. *The Social Body: Habit, Identity and Desire*. Thousand Oaks, CA: Sage.

Currier, D. M. 2013. "Strategic Ambiguity: Protecting Emphasized Femininity and Hegemonic Masculinity in the Hookup Culture." *Gender & Society* 27 (5): 704–27.

Darwin, H. 2017. "Doing Gender beyond the Binary." *Symbolic Interaction* 40 (3): 317–34.

Davis, G. 2015. *Contesting Intersex: The Dubious Diagnosis*. New York: New York University Press.

de Beauvoir, S. (1949) 1972. *The Second Sex*. Translated by H. M. Parshley. New York: Penguin. Citations refer to the 1972 translation.

D'Emilio, J. 1993. "Capitalism and Gay Identity." In *The Lesbian and Gay Studies Reader*, edited by H. Abelove, M. A. Barale, and D. M. Halperin, 467–78. London: Routledge.

Desmond, M. 2006. "Becoming a Firefighter." *Ethnography* 7 (4): 387–421.

Diefendorf, S., and T. Bridges. 2020. "On the Enduring Relationship between Masculinity and Homophobia." *Sexualities* 23 (7): 1264–84.

Dill, B. T. 1988. "Our Mothers' Grief: Racial Ethnic Women and the Maintenance of Families." *Journal of Family History* 13 (1): 415–31.

Domeneghetti, R. 2017. "'The Other Side of the Net': (Re)presentations of (Emphasised) Femininity during Wimbledon 2016." *Journal of Policy Research in Tourism, Leisure and Events* 10, no. 2 (November): 1–13.

Dowsett, G. 1996. *Practicing Desire: Homosexual Sex in the Era of Aids*. Stanford, CA: Stanford University Press.

Dozier, R. 2005. "Beards, Breasts, and Bodies: Doing Sex in a Gendered World." *Gender & Society* 19 (3): 297–316.

Dreger, A. 1998. *Hermaphrodites and the Medical Invention of Sex*. Cambridge, MA: Harvard University Press.

Dworkin, A. 1980. "Pornography and Grief." In *Take Back the Night*, edited by L. Lederer. New York: William Morrow.

Echols, A. 1989. *Daring to Be Bad: Radical Feminism in America, 1967–1975*. Minneapolis: University of Minnesota Press.

Eisenstein, H. 1983. *Contemporary Feminist Thought*. Boston: Hall.

Eisenstein, Z. R. 1979. *Capitalist Patriarchy and the Case for Socialist Feminism*. New York: Monthly Review Press.

Engels, F. (1884) 1942. *The Origin of the Family, Private Property, and the State*. Translated by A. West. New York: International Publishers. Citations refer to the 1942 translation.

Epstein, C. F. 1988. *Deceptive Distinctions: Sex, Gender and the Social Order*. New Haven, CT: Yale University Press.

Fausto-Sterling, A. 2000. *Sexing the Body: Gender Politics and the Construction of Sexuality*. New York: Basic.

Firestone, S. 1970. *The Dialectic of Sex*. New York: William Morrow.

Foucault, M. 1979. *Discipline and Punish: The Birth of the Prison*. New York: Vintage.

———. 1980. *Herculine Barbin*. New York: Vintage.

Garfinkel, H. 1967. *Studies in Ethnomethodology*. Englewood Cliffs, NJ: Prentice Hall.

Garcia, L. 2012. *Respect Yourself, Protect Yourself: Latina Girls and Sexual Identity*. New York: New York University Press.

Garrison, S. 2018. "On the Limits of 'Trans Enough': Authenticating Trans Identity Narratives." *Gender & Society* 32 (5): 613–37.

Giddens, A. 1976. *New Rules of Sociological Method: A Positive Critique of Interpretive Sociologies.* New York: Basic.

———. 1984. *The Constitution of Society.* Berkeley: University of California Press.

———. 1991. *Modernity and Self Identity.* Stanford, CA: Stanford University Press.

Goffman, E. 1963. *Behavior in Public Places.* New York: Free Press.

———. 1968. *Stigma.* Englewood Cliffs, NJ: Prentice Hall.

———. 1972. *Relations in Public.* New York: Harper & Row.

———. 1979. *Gender Advertisements.* New York: Harper & Row.

Gutmann, M. 2019. *Are Men Animals? How Modern Masculinity Sells Men Short.* New York: Basic.

Hames-Garcia, M. 2011. *Identity Complex: Making the Case for Multiplicity.* Minneapolis: University of Minnesota Press.

Hamilton, J. 2020. "Undoing Gender or Overdoing Gender? Women MMA Athletes' Intimate Partnering and the Relational Maintenance of Femininity." *Sociology of Sport Journal* 37 (4): 346–54.

Hartmann, H. 1981. "The Unhappy Marriage of Marxism and Feminism: Toward a More Progressive Union." In *Women and Revolution*, edited by L. Sargent. Boston: South End Press.

Heaton, J. 2004. *Reworking Qualitative Data.* Thousand Oaks, CA: Sage.

Hechavarria, D. M., and A. E. Ingram. 2016. "The Entrepreneurial Divide: Hegemonic Masculinity, Emphasized Femininity and Organizational Forms." *International Journal of Gender and Entrepreneurship* 8 (3): 242–81.

Hollander, J. A. 2013. "'I Demand More of People': Accountability, Interaction, and Gender Change." *Gender & Society* 27 (1): 5–29.

———. 2018. "Interactional Accountability." In *Handbook of the Sociology of Gender*, 2nd ed., edited by B. J. Risman, C. M. Froyum, and W. J. Scarborough, 173–84. Cham, Switzerland: Springer.

Holstein, J. A., and J. F. Gubrium. 1995. *The Active Interview.* Thousand Oaks, CA: Sage.

Hoskin, R. A. 2017. "Femme Theory: Refocusing the Intersectional Lens." *Atlantis* 38 (1): 95–109.

———. 2019. "Femmephobia: The Role of Anti-femininity and Gender Policing in LGBTQ+ People's Experiences of Discrimination." *Sex Roles* 81: 686–703.

———. 2020. "'Femininity? It's the Aesthetic of Subordination': Examining Femmephobia, the Gender Binary, and Experiences of Oppression among Sexual and Gender Minorities." *Archives of Sexual Behavior* 49: 2319–39.

Hoskin, R. A., and K. L. Blair. 2021. "Critical Femininities: A 'New' Approach to Gender Theory." *Psychology & Sexuality* 13: 1–8.

Ispa-Landa, S., and M. Oliver. 2020. "Hybrid Femininities: Making Sense of Sorority Rankings and Reputation." *Gender & Society* 34 (6): 893–921.

Jackson, S. 2007. "The Sexual Self in Late Modernity." In *The Sexual Self*, edited by M. Kimmel, 3–15. Nashville, TN: Vanderbilt University Press.

Jackson, S., and S. Scott. 2010. *Theorizing Sexuality.* New York: McGraw-Hill.

Jaggar, A. 1983. *Feminist Politics and Human Nature.* Totowa, NJ: Rowman & Littlefield.

Katz, J. N. 1990. "The Invention of Heterosexuality." *Socialist Review* 20 (January–March): 7–34.

Ken, I. 2010. *Digesting Race, Class, and Gender: Sugar as a Metaphor.* Basingstoke: Palgrave Macmillan.

Ken, I., and A. S. Helmuth. 2021. "Not Additive, Not Defined: Mutual Constitution in Feminist Intersectional Studies." *Feminist Theory* 22 (4): 575–604.

Kessler, S., D. J. Ashenden, R. W. Connell, and G. W. Dowsett. 1982. *Ockers and Disco-Maniacs.* Sydney: Inner City Education Center.

Kessler, S. J. 1990. "The Medical Construction of Gender: Case Management of Intersexed Infants." *Signs* 16 (1): 3–26.

———. 2002. *Lessons from the Intersexed.* New Brunswick, NJ: Rutgers University Press.

Kessler, S. J., and W. McKenna. 1978. *Gender: An Ethnomethodological Approach.* New York: John Wiley.

King, D. K. 1988. "Multiple Jeopardy, Multiple Consciousness: The Context of Black Feminist Ideology." *Signs* 14 (1): 42–72.

Kitzinger, C. 2005. "Speaking as a Heterosexual: (How) Does Sexuality Matter for Talk-in-Interaction?" *Research on Language and Social Interaction* 38 (3): 221–65.

Klein, J. 2013. *The Bully Society.* New York: New York University Press.

Kostas, M. 2019. "Discursive Construction of Hegemonic Masculinity and Emphasized Femininity in Textbooks of Primary Education: Children's Discursive Agency and Polysemy of the Narratives." *Gender and Education* 33 (1): 50–67.

Laqueur, T. 1990. *Making Sex: Body and Gender from the Greeks to Freud.* Cambridge, MA: Harvard University Press.

Lorber, J. 1994. *Paradoxes of Gender.* New Haven, CT: Yale University Press.

———. 2018. "Paradoxes of Gender Redux: Multiple Genders and the Persistence of the Binary." In *Gender Reckonings: New Social Theory and Research*, edited by J. W. Messerschmidt, P. Martin, M. Messner, and R. Connell. New York: New York University Press.

———. 2022. *The New Gender Paradox: Fragmentation and Persistence of the Binary.* Cambridge: Polity Press.

Lorber, J., and L. J. Moore. 2011. *Gendered Bodies.* 2nd ed. New York: Oxford University Press.

Lucal, B. 1999. "What It Means to Be Gendered Me: Life on the Boundaries of a Dichotomous Gender System." *Gender & Society* 13 (6): 781–97.

MacKinnon, C. 1982. "Feminism, Marxism, Method, and the State: An Agenda for Theory." *Signs* 7 (3): 515–44.

———. 1989. *Toward a Feminist Theory of the State.* Cambridge, MA: Harvard University Press.

Martin, K. 2018. *Puberty, Sexuality and the Self: Girls and Boys at Adolescence.* New York and London: Routledge.

Martin, P. Y. 2001. "'Mobilizing Masculinities': Men's Experiences of Women at Work." *Organizations* 8 (4): 587–618.

———. 2003. "'Said and Done' versus 'Saying and Doing': Gendering Practices, Practicing Gender at Work." *Gender & Society* 17 (3): 342–66.

———. 2004. "Gender as Social Institution." *Social Forces* 82: 1249–73.

———. 2006. "Practicing Gender at Work: Further Thoughts on Reflexivity." *Gender, Work and Organization* 13 (3): 254–76.

Matthews, J. J. 1984. *Good and Mad Women: The Historical Construction of Femininity in Twentieth-Century Australia.* Sydney: Allen & Unwin.

Mead, M. 1935. *Sex and Temperament in Three Primitive Societies.* New York: William Morrow and Co.

Meadow, T. 2010. "'A Rose Is a Rose': On Producing Legal Gender Classifications." *Gender & Society* 24 (6): 814–37.

———. 2018. *Trans Kids.* Berkeley: University of California Press.

Messerschmidt, J. W. 2000. *Nine Lives: Adolescent Masculinities, the Body, and Violence.* Boulder, CO: Westview.

———. 2004. *Flesh & Blood: Adolescent Gender Diversity and Violence.* Lanham, MD: Rowman & Littlefield.

———. 2010. *Hegemonic Masculinities and Camouflaged Politics.* Boulder, CO: Paradigm.

———. 2012. *Gender, Heterosexuality, and Youth Violence: The Struggle for Recognition.* Lanham, MD: Rowman & Littlefield.

———. 2014. *Crime as Structured Action.* 2nd ed. Lanham, MD: Rowman & Littlefield.

———. 2016. *Masculinities in the Making: From the Local to the Global.* Lanham, MD: Rowman & Littlefield.

———. 2018a. *Hegemonic Masculinity: Formulation, Reformulation, and Amplification.* Lanham, MD: Rowman & Littlefield.

———. 2018b. *Masculinities and Crime: A Quarter Century of Theory and Research.* 25th anniversary ed. Lanham, MD: Rowman & Littlefield.

Millett, K. 1970. *Sexual Politics.* New York: Doubleday.

Mitchell, J. 1966. "Women: The Longest Revolution." *New Left Review* 40: 11–37.

———. 1971. *Women's Estate.* New York: Penguin.

Mohanty, C. T. 1988. "Under Western Eyes: Feminist Scholarship and Colonial Discourse." *Feminist Review* 30: 61–88.

Mora, R. 2012. "'Doing It for Your Pubic Hairs!' Latino Boys, Masculinity, and Puberty." *Gender & Society* 26 (3): 433–60.

Morgan, D. 1992. *Discovering Men.* New York: Routledge.

Morgan, R. 1978. *Going Too Far.* New York: Random House.

Nadal, K. L., C. N. Whitman, L. S. Davis, T. Erazo, and K. C. Davidoff. 2016. "Microaggressions toward Lesbian, Gay, Bisexual, Transgender, Queer, and Genderqueer People: A Review of the Literature." *Journal of Sex Research* 53 (4–5): 488–508.

Nestle, J., C. Howell, and R. Wilchins, eds. 2020. *Genderqueer: Voices beyond the Sexual Binary.* 2nd ed. Riverdale, NY: Riverdale Avenue Books.

Nisar, M. A. 2017. "(Un)Becoming a Man: Legal Consciousness of the Third Gender Category in Pakistan." *Gender & Society* 32 (1): 59–81.

Oakley, A. 1972. *Sex, Gender, and Society.* San Francisco, CA: Harper & Row.

Omi, M., and H. Winant. 1994. *Racial Formations in the United States from the 1960s to the 1990s*. New York and London: Routledge.

Orbuch, T. 1997. "People's Accounts Count: The Sociology of Accounts." *Annual Review of Sociology* 23: 455–78.

Ozyegin, G. 2018. "Rethinking Patriarchy through Unpatriarchal Male Desires." In *Gender Reckonings: New Social Theory and Research*, edited by J. W. Messerschmidt, P. Martin, M. Messner, and R. Connell. New York: New York University Press.

Paechter, C. 2006. "Masculine Femininities/Feminine Masculinities: Power, Identities, and Gender." *Gender and Education* 18 (3): 253–63.

Pascoe, C. J. 2007. *Dude, You're a Fag: Masculinity and Sexuality in High School.* Berkeley: University of California Press.

———. 2013. "Notes on a Sociology of Bullying: Young Men's Homophobia as Gender Socialization." *QED: A Journal of GLBTQ Worldmaking* 1: 87–104.

Patton, M. Q. 1990. *Qualitative Evaluation and Research Methods*. Newbury Park, CA: Sage.

Pfeffer, C. A. 2012. "Normative Resistance and Inventive Pragmatism: Negotiating Structure and Agency in Transgender Families." *Gender & Society* 26 (4): 574–602.

———. 2014. "'I Don't Like Passing as a Straight Woman': Queer Negotiations of Identity and Social Group Membership." *American Journal of Sociology* 120 (1): 1–44.

Preves, S. 2004. *Intersex and Identity: The Contested Self*. New Brunswick, NJ: Rutgers University Press.

Rich, A. 1976. *Of Woman Born*. New York: Norton.

Richards, C., W. P. Bouman, and M-J. Barker, eds. 2017. *Genderqueer and Non-binary Genders.* London: Palgrave Macmillan.

Risman, B. J. 2004. "Gender as a Social Structure: Theory, Wrestling with Activism." *Gender & Society* 18 (4): 429–50.

———. 2018a. "Gender as a Social Structure." In *Handbook of the Sociology of Gender*, 2nd ed., edited by B. J. Risman, C. M. Froyum, and W. J. Scarborough, 19–43. New York: New York University Press.

———. 2018b. *Where the Millennials Will Take Us: A New Generation Wrestles with the Gender Structure*. New York: Oxford University Press.

Risman, B. J., K. Myers, and R. Sin. 2018. "Limitations of the Neoliberal Turn in Gender Theory: (Re)Turning to Gender as a Social Structure." In *Gender Reckonings: New Social Theory and Research*, edited by J. W. Messerschmidt, P. Martin, M. Messner, and R. Connell. New York: New York University Press.

Rowbotham, S. 1973. *Women's Consciousness, Man's World.* New York: Penguin.

———. 1981. "The Trouble with 'Patriarchy.'" In *People's History and Socialist Theory*, edited by S. Raphael. Boston: Routledge & Kegan Paul.

Saffioti, H. I. B. 1978. *Women in Class Society.* New York: Monthly Review Press.

Saguy, A. C., and J. A. Williams. 2022. "A Little Word That Means a Lot: A Reassessment of Singular *They* in a New Era of Gender Politics." *Gender & Society* 36 (1): 5–31.

Sartre, J. P. 1956. *Being and Nothingness.* Translated by H. E. Barnes. New York: Washington Square Press.

Schegloff, E. A. 1986. "The Routine as Achievement." *Human Studies* 9: 111–51.

Schilt, K. 2010. *Just One of the Guys? Transgender Men and the Persistence of Gender Inequality.* Chicago: University of Chicago Press.

Schilt, K., and L. Westbrook. 2009. "Doing Gender, Doing Heteronormativity: 'Gender Normals,' Transgender People, and the Social Maintenance of Heterosexuality." *Gender & Society* 23 (4): 440–64.

Schilt, K., and E. Windsor. 2014. "The Sexual Habitus of Transgender Men: Negotiating Sexuality through Gender." *Journal of Homosexuality* 61 (5): 732–48.

Schippers, M. 2007. "Recovering the Feminine Other: Masculinity, Femininity, and Gender Hegemony." *Theory & Society* 36 (1): 85–102.

Seccombe, W. 1973. "The Housewife and Her Labour under Capitalism." *New Left Review* 83 (1): 3–24.

Sedgwick, E. K. 1995. "Gosh Boy George, You Must Be Awfully Secure in Your Masculinity." In *Constructing Masculinity*, edited by M. Berger, B. Wallis, and S. Watson, 11–20. New York and London: Routledge.

Seidman, S. 2010. *The Social Construction of Sexuality.* 2nd ed. New York: Norton.

shuster, s. m. 2017. "Punctuating Accountability: How Discursive Aggression Regulates Transgender People." *Gender & Society* 31 (4): 481–502.

Silva, J. M. 2008. "A New Generation of Women? How Female ROTC Cadets Negotiate the Tension between Masculine Military Culture and Traditional Femininity." *Social Forces* 87 (2): 937–60.

Spellman, E. V. 1988. *Inessential Woman: Problems of Exclusion in Feminist Thought.* Boston: Beacon.

Stacey, J., and B. Thorne. 1985. "The Missing Feminist Revolution in Sociology." *Social Problems* 32 (4): 301–16.

Stoller, R. 1968. *Sex and Gender: On the Development of Masculinity and Femininity.* New York: Science House.

Strauss, A., and J. Corbin. 1998. *Basics of Qualitative Research.* Thousand Oaks, CA: Sage.

Talbot, K., and M. Quayle. 2010. "The Perils of Being a Nice Guy: Contextual Variation in Five Young Women's Constructions of Acceptable Hegemonic and Alternative Masculinities." *Men and Masculinities* 13 (2): 255–78.

Tapley, H. 2013. "Queering Paradise: Toni Morrison's Anti-capitalist Production." *Feminist Theory* 14 (1): 21–37.

Thomas, W. I., and F. Znaniecki. (1927) 1958. *The Polish Peasant in Europe and America.* New York: Dover.

Thorne, B. 1993. *Gender Play: Girls and Boys in School.* New Brunswick, NJ: Rutgers University Press.

Tolman, D.L. 1994. "Doing Desire: Adolescent Girls' Struggles for/with Sexuality." *Gender & Society* 8 (3): 324–42.

Valerio, A. M., and K. Sawyer. 2016. "The Men Who Mentor Women." *Harvard Business Review*, December 6, 2016, 1–7.

Walby, S. 1986. *Patriarchy at Work.* Minneapolis: University of Minnesota Press.

Weeks, J. 1986. *Sexuality.* London and New York: Routledge.

West, C., and S. Fenstermaker. 1995. "Doing Difference." *Gender & Society* 9 (1): 8–37.

West, C., and D. Zimmerman. 1987. "Doing Gender." *Gender & Society* 1 (2): 125–51.

———. 2009. "Accounting for Doing Gender." *Gender & Society* 23 (1): 112–22.

Westbrook, L., and K. Schilt. 2014. "Doing Gender, Determining Gender: Transgender People, Gender Panics, and the Maintenance of the Sex/Gender/Sexuality System." *Gender & Society* 28 (1): 32–57.

Willer, R., C. L. Rogalin, B. Conlon, and M. T. Wojnowicz. 2013. "Overdoing Gender: A Test of the Masculine Overcompensation Thesis." *American Journal of Sociology* 118 (4): 980–1022.

Wolkomir, M. 2012. "'You Fold Like a Little Girl': (Hetero)Gender Framing and Competitive Strategies of Men and Women in No Limit Texas Hold Em Poker Games." *Qualitative Sociology* 35: 407–26.

Worthen, M. G. F. 2020. *Queers, Bis, and Straight Lies: An Intersectional Examination of LGBTQ Stigma.* New York: Routledge.

———. 2021. "Why Can't You Just Pick One? The Stigmatization of Non-binary/Genderqueer People by Cis and Trans Men and Women: An Empirical Test of Norm-Centered Stigma Theory." *Sex Roles* 85: 343–56.

Young, I. M. 1990. *Throwing Like a Girl, and Other Essays in Feminist Philosophy and Social Theory.* Bloomington: Indiana University Press.

Index

About the Authors

James W. Messerschmidt is distinguished university professor emeritus of sociology at the University of Southern Maine, where he taught for thirty-five years. In addition to more than eighty research articles and book chapters, Messerschmidt authored fifteen books, most recently, *Hegemonic Masculinity: Formulation, Reformulation, and Amplification* (2018) and *Gender Reckonings: New Social Theory and Research* (2018; coedited with Patricia Yancey Martin, Michael Messner, and Raewyn Connell). His research interests focus on cognitive sociology; inequalities; the mutual constitution of identities; gender, masculinities, and sexualities; criminology, youth crime, and violence; and political sociology.

Tristan Bridges is associate professor of sociology at the University of California, Santa Barbara. He is coeditor of the Sage journal *Men and Masculinities* and coeditor of *Exploring Masculinities: Identity, Inequality, Continuity, and Change* (2016). His research is broadly concerned with shifts in gender and sexual identities and inequalities with a focus on masculinity. Bridges has conducted research with bodybuilders, fathers' rights activists, pro-feminist men, and bar regulars, and on gendered demographic shifts in sexual minority identities in the United States, the relationship between American masculinity and mass shootings, and gendered anxieties present in search data on Google.com. He lives in Goleta, California, with his family.

www.ingramcontent.com/pod-product-compliance
Lightning Source LLC
Chambersburg PA
CBHW031137270326
41929CB00011B/1660